Collected Essays

Collected Essays

Dr. Sukhamoy Ghosh

ALLIED PUBLISHERS PVT. LTD.

Noida • Mumbai • Kolkata • Chennai • Bangalore

ALLIED PUBLISHERS PRIVATE LIMITED

D-5, Sector-2, **Noida**–201 301
Ph. Nos.: 0120-4320295/2542557/4352866
E-mail: delhi.books@alliedpublishers.com

17 Chittaranjan Avenue, **Kolkata**–700072
Ph.: 033-22129618 • E-mail: cal.books@alliedpublishers.com

15 J.N. Heredia Marg, Ballard Estate, **Mumbai**–400001
Ph.: 022-42126969 • E-mail: mumbai.books@alliedpublishers.com

No. 25/10, Commander-in-Chief Road, Ethiraj Lane (Next to Post Office)
Egmore, **Chennai**–600008
Ph.: 044-28223938 • E-mail: chennai.books@alliedpublishers.com

P.B. No. 9932, No. 15, 3rd Floor (Next to Vijaya Bank), 5th Cross, Gandhinagar, Karnataka, **Bangalore**–560009. Ph.: 080-41530285 / 22386239
E-mail: bngl.journals@alliedpublishers.com / apsabng@airtelmail.in

Website: www.alliedpublishers.com

ISBN: 978-93-90951-94-9

Published by Sunil Sachdev and printed by Ravi Sachdev
at Allied Publishers Pvt. Ltd., D-5, Sector-2, Noida–201 301

Preface

The present collection of essays by Mr. S. Ghosh , my grandfather primarily presents philosophical dissertations on man's appreciation of the world around him through various means, ranging from the use of language to approximating it by action, from a common man's motivation behind his work to that of a monk, who is supposed to be free from all attachments and so on.

The author's basic idea is that in all kinds of man's activities involving his world along with others', mind is at the centre of everything. By way of deliberating on this aspect of man, Mr. Ghosh has talked about human psychology on many occasions, though in his rational way of approach. But it is this approach of the author that can interest a scholar who works in the field of Psychology to say a few words.

In his 'The Karma Principle of the Gita and the Nature of Human action', for example, Mr. Ghosh quotes from Freud's 'Beyond the Pleasure Principle' to write: Looking from this psychological point of view, the proposition that 'man by nature cannot but constantly act towards improving his state' does no longer remain improbable. Rather this becomes his identity as a being who, no matter under what conditions, does so.

Again, in 'Meaning, Concept and Compromise', regarding the role of mind in man's reaching on to the world around him, he writes: ..." what we shall see that the word 'concept' used by Russell has not been amply analysed and that if it were so analysed, ... we would see that the word 'concept' is a very 'notorious' customer in the process of communication.... It involves several elements including a person's mental structure and his world of experience...."

From what I have garnered from my little pursuit in the field of Psychology so far, I would say that the brain can be likened to that of a plastic mould, capable of being altered and shaped. Neuroplasticity, in itself, is the brain's ability to change or adapt over time, by generating new neurons and assembling new networks. (*Neuroplasticity | Psychology Today*, n.d.). This concept of neuroplasticity directly aligns with the author's endorsement of how 'man by nature cannot but constantly act towards improving his state', where the brain's malleability renders it structurally capable of changing as a result of learning.

In "Argument for a Higher Life of the Common Man" he writes: "... every man is a common man in the sense he is part of Nature's continuous process of evolving out of more and more congenial states in its different fields, where noncompliance of this means extinction. And the equivalent of this process in 'human field' is evolving a higher state of life. .... He cannot but follow this course of the process."

Although it was once believed that the brain remained fixed after an individual reached a certain age, contemporary research suggests that the brain never ceases to change in response to learning (Chen *et al.*, 2020). Thus it is through man being constant learners do we evolve and have the ability to even change the physical structure of our brain.

From this point of view, I can ascertain that these essays add an important shade to the inner workings of the human mind.

Teachers College,
Columbia University. NY

Rhiya Ghosh
September 2023

Contents

What is in a Sentence !*

1. It Facilitates Awareness and Communication

A sentence is not just another section in the learner's Grammar book. It is the articulated form of a statement made by a person about a fact of the world without performing which neither the person making it can get to the fact himself, nor can he present the fact to anyone else whom he intends to apprise. The former makes possible the person's own awareness of the fact, the latter makes possible *communicating* the meaning of the sentence by a speaker (who may also be a writer, or any of its substitute), to a hearer (or a reader or any of such recipient) the speaker might intend. It is obvious that the language in which one makes it for himself is one he accesses. It is equally essential for the sentence he makes by way of uttering for the sake of communication for the hearer who accesses. This act works only in a common field of accessibility by both the two parties in question. [There may be cases where the sentence is put to work in a field where the two do not belong to common field. What happens in such cases, we shall see later.]

The function that a sentence plays is that, it states 'something is so and so' ('s is p') referring to a state of affairs of the world such that something-is-so-and-so. For example, the sentence 'The table is brown' states that 'something (the table) is so and so (is brown)' referring to a state of affairs of the world, namely, a 'brown-table'. As for awareness of the maker himself, the components of the sentence, namely, words, may not be explicitly articulated but in essence their use is there as his awareness progresses in his thought. But if it comes

* Revised version of the Author's "Are all sentences communicative?" *Indian Philosophical Quarterly*. Vol. VII, No. 3, April 1981.

to communicating to another, the components explicitly make the sentence so that the hearer can access it.

A man has awareness of his own thoughts or beliefs, his feeling or emotions, his pleasure, pain, fear or anxiety, in short, all of his mental states, only when he finds a suitable form of sentence for it. For example, when one is happy, his happiness is realised by him only by going through a mental state of the form 'I am so happy' (that is, stating that 'something is so and so') without which form, expressed or unexpressed, he himself cannot see the state of his mind. In other words, a suitable sentence form is the only carrier of his awareness to him.

Similarly, when he intends to communicate the same awareness to another person or persons, he makes it extra-mental by way of, say, uttering some words. This latter act takes the expressed form (uttered, written, or the like) of the above sentence ('I am so happy') to communicate its *meaning* (i.e. the state it represents or refers to) to the intended person.

The expressed form of the communicative act does not always take the same form. For example, if one can speak, he makes some sounds what are generally words to make the sentence. If he cannot speak, for example, if he is deaf and dumb, or is required not to make any sound, he uses movement of his limbs, may be eyes, fingers, head etc. or even by drawing some pictures (not words, due to incompetence or for other reasons) with this belief that this kind of act shall communicate his mental state to the person or persons he intends. But nevertheless all these make some form of a sentence in such communication.

Thus, for one's own awareness or for communicating the same to someone else, this act of finding a sentence is a must in every case whether he is sad, looks at a table for its colour, is admiring the beauty of Sunset on a mountain peak, or appreciates the proceedings of the play 'Romeo and Juliet'. The difference is, it is the carrier of awareness to oneself, and of 'something' as its *meaning* to another.

In the sections to follow, we shall be dealing with this communicative role of a sentence.

2. Its Communicative Function has a Definite Pattern

A sentence for communication is generally made of words (overt or covert). There may be other forms, as stated above, used as a tool of communication, but such forms to be communicative must be transformed into the form of a sentence.

What the speaker communicates to the hearer is said to be the 'meaning' of the sentence the former intends to communicate. Unintentional utterance of words or a substitute of it in any other form does not make a sentence under the present agenda. The way a sentence communicates its meaning to another person may be explained with an example.

As for the speech module, let us refer to a case where one looks at a table and utters a sentence (S): 'The table is brown'. Here he utters four words, namely, 'The, 'table', 'is', and 'brown', representing respectively 'a definite article to refer to a particular object', 'a substantive, i.e. an object (of a particular name)', 'a relation of being pervaded by ', and 'a quality'. Here the words all together 'work' in a particular manner (grammatical or otherwise) to make the sentence (S) which makes a statement 's is p' that refers to a fact (f). Here the f is the 'Brown-Table' (let us call it Bt) which, along with other facts of the world, make, in the words of Wittgenstein: 'the world that is the case'.

This 'referring act' makes the sentence meaningful, because this finds the S either referring favourably, that is, the S is found true (T) or unfavourably, that is, the S is found false (F). If there is Bt there, the above S is T, and the sentence s is meaningful. If it is '–Bt', the above S is F but again the S is meaningful to ascertain it as false.

Thus we find that a meaningful sentence is the one which as an utterance works only through this pattern of "S 's-p' f(T/F)" which means: a sentence states a S that refers to a fact or state of affair f such that the S can be known as T or F. Non-working of this pattern makes an utterance a meaningless or a non-sense act.

It may be noted here that, a word (or a sign transformed into word) does not individually refer to some 'f' for T/F. It has a 'feature' that makes it competent to be used in the sentence for stating a S such that it, along with other similar words, can refer to a f. In that sense, a word occurring in a sentence may be said to have a feature of the intended f. Let us call such words, words having 'f^{fe}'. Only the occurrence of such words in a particular manner (i.e. a relation), whereby it becomes a sentence that states a s-p referring to f. The sentence 'The table is brown' involves such words that, as shown above, have competence, by their individual f^{fe}, to make the respective S to refer to the f. On the other hand, a so-called sentence "An abracad homogenets Abracadum "uses a few sounds like 'Abracad', 'homogenets', and 'Abracadum', which appear like words but have no f^{fe} (because they do not have any defined feature that belongs to any state of affair of the world) do not make a sentence of communicative pattern of "S 's-p' f(T/F)". Such sentence-like utterances do not make a sentence of meaning.

> [Sentence-like utterances (or writings, etc.) of the above kind, if intentional, are not, however, without any meaning-value. But such value is different from that of sentences of normal use. Shall be discussed when we come to that].

About how the words occur in a sentence, it may be said, not all sentences are like the overtly uttered one like 'The table is brown'. There may be cases where such words occur only covertly, or occur without being in the required grammatical form. For example, a person replying to a question by another regarding whether he believes in God, says 'Yes'. Here the single word overtly uttered has two or four more possible covert companions to complete the sentence that communicates the meaning of the S for the referring act, namely, 'I', and 'do'; or, 'I', 'believe', 'in', and 'God', or the like, as the case may be.

Similarly, there may be other forms of utterances where the sentence form that spells a statement for the referring act is not observed. For example, a person A commands: 'Come here!'. It does not take the usual sentence form that states something. Yet the hearer B gets the meaning of it. Otherwise such commands would have gone un-responded as 'meaningless sounds'. It is meaningful because it delivers an implicit sentence, namely, "This is an order to make one (here for whom uttered) go towards the speaker", or the like. And the sentence S states 'the speaker's order is such and such', which, like any other S stated by a sentence refers to a state of affair for the hearer, namely, 'order-to-go-towards, etc.' Here the f is not a physical entity but a 'conceivable situation'. [Later we shall see that for the sake of meaning what the s-p of a sentence refers to is not a physical entity as such, but a 'concept' about it.]

Again, so far use of words are concerned, there may be cases where communication is performed with no words at use at all. For example, a tribesman of the North-east Forest Region of India are sometimes found to make a kind of sound by beating drums in a particular manner with the intention that it reaches the ears of the inhabitants in the neighbourhood with the intended message. In such an exercise what the neighbours hear is not just the sound of the beating of drum, but a message in the sentence form which says 'Alert all ! A rogue is sighted nearby'. This is done by a process of transformation (by the hearer) at the instance of 'competent materials' provided by the intending maker. This process of transformation to a sentence takes place whenever such competent materials are produced, be it in a painting, through movement of limb, or by any other act for the purpose.

In this connection it may also be remembered that, the sentence shall do its work (awareness and communication) if only the right components are chosen to form it. If it is not so done, it causes a 'non-working' condition for the speaker providing 'wrong awareness', and for the hearer, a 'wrong meaning'. For example, if a speaker makes a S 'There is a snake' for a 'rope', which happens in illusions, it causes wrong awareness for him. For the hearer, however, it is 'meaningful' as F. If, on the other hand, a speaker utters 'That is a post' to refer to a pillar, and the hearer takes the word 'post' for another state of affair, say, a post (from post office), (also another f^{fe} of the word 'post'), then for the hearer the S states a s-p that is F, and hence 'meaningful', but practically he is wrong, for, this meaning was not intended by the sentence.

3. Its Meaning is in its Referring

It may be said that a sentence that communicates is not mere words or signs/sounds making it, but an act that conveys some 'meaning', by stating a S which, with reference to a fact or a 'state of affairs' (of the world), is either true or false (T/F), depending on whether the S made by it (of the form 's is p' or 's is not-p') corresponds or does not correspond to the fact (f) referred. Thus, if the S 'the table is brown' stated by the sentence favourably corresponds to what it refers to, that means where the fact is also 'Bt' (Brown-Table), then the S of the sentence is true. If on the other hand, the fact is a 'white table' (Wt, that is, -Bt), then the S is false taking the form 's is not-p'. But in both cases the sentence is meaningful.[1] Meaning of a sentence stating 's is not p' follows the same pattern of reference.

Similarly, if the neighbours, of the instance mentioned earlier, find the trace of an elephant, that is to say, find that the meaning of the message corresponds to the referred fact, namely, 'EN' (elephant-in- neighbourhood), the meaning of the sentence (here the message of the drum beating) is communicated since the S it states ('s is p' or 'There is an elephant'), is true. If, again, there are no elephants (that means, if the fact is '-EN'), the S of the message-sentence mentioned above (namely, 's is p') is meaningful as false. And when this falsity

[1] Here one thing may be noted. The unfavourable correspondence of S also says that a contrary of it, namely, a sentence stating – S is meaningful as T.

is understood, there is simultaneously understood another sentence conveying the former's opposite meaning by stating a S 'No elephant is sighted', which is true.

What we have observed in the above is that, a sentence to communicate, some meaning must state something that corresponds to some fact. This correspondence may be favourable (where the S is true) or unfavourable (where the S is false), both making the sentence meaningful. But in any case, the st (the statement) of the sentence S must refer to some fact ('f') of the world to perform this act of correspondence such that it is either T or F.

Let us consider here a few questions that may be asked about this meaning-function, that is, *referring* to see how the f, referred to, corresponds. Does a sentence uttered/written (or a transformed one from some relevant act), must necessarily follow this 'S s-p f(T/F)' pattern? If that is the case, then for a sentence to be meaningful, there must be some f (some state of affair of the world) to correspond.

But there may be 'sentences' (that is, some act of making sentences in the stated sense) which are 'meaningful' but do not at all refer to any fact of the world in the sense stated above.

Let us refer to two kinds of sentences, namely, (1) Those that are used in a fiction; and (2) Those that some philosophical thinkers use. Both may be seen to use sentences that mean imagined (or thought of) 'facts' and hence no question of their corresponding to facts of the world favourably or unfavourably. Nevertheless, both kinds of sentences are treated as perfectly meaningful, the latter rather claiming that such sentences are subject of ultimate human understanding.

As for fictional sentence, one of the stories in Aesop's Fable begins with this sentence: 'There was once an argument between the wind and the sun...'. Here the sentence means that the wind and the sun are engaged in an 'argument', such that the S cannot correspond to a state of affair (whether favourably or unfavourably), because neither wind nor sun are speaking species, no question being in argument. So the S of the sentence fails to fulfil the criterion of correspondence to make it meaningful. But the sentence does communicate a 'meaning' and the reader receives it as perfectly corresponding to a situation ('state of affair') where 'the wind speaks and is in argument with the sun who too is doing the same'.

The communicative function of a sentence in its usual pattern, as we have seen, is: 'S s-p f(T/F)', whereas, in the above case we find that the referring act is wilfully construed by the reader pushing aside its state of affair claim (as of Wittgenstein's) in order to get to the pleasure as well as to the message of the story. In literary discipline we call it 'wilful suspension of disbelief'. That means, meaning of a sentence is a 'product of compromise by acceptance'. In one sense, therefore, there may be sentences the communicated meaning of which is 'acceptance' by the hearer (or the reader etc.) as 'corresponding' to the referred f even by suspended disbelief.

As for philosophical systems, sometimes we find sentences the meaning of which is not accessible on the basis of their reference to facts. In fact, they refer to 'something' which is not 'f' in our sense, whether actual or possible.

For example, the sentence used by the advocates of Vedanta philosophy to designate the ultimate reality of the universe (i.e. Brahman) is: "He (Brahman) transcends all attributes", which means, "Brahman cannot be determined by any qualities. Brahman is indeterminate (anirvacaniya)". A somewhat similar statement was made by Kant when he referred to the "things-in-themselves' of the universe by using the term 'Noumena' saying: 'A thing-in-itself is unknown and unknowable'. These sentences do not state S's to refer to facts ('f') of the world. As for the Vedanta sentence, it states something like 's (the subject) has an attribute (p) which transcends all attributes', that is, s is attributed by 'no-attribute', which is a simple contradiction in terms. So the S of this philosophical sentence cannot perform any correspondence act. And since without this correspondence it can nether be true nor false, it fails the mark of being meaningful. Similarly knowing the 'unknowable' is self-contradictory. Failing the required criteria, therefore, these sentences should be declared as 'meaningless'. But the exponents of these philosophical statements showed that it is the very way that the Ultimate Truth of the universe can be stated. That opens for a different kind of deliberation. Presently we are concerned with another important condition, demanded by it, that needs to be fulfilled before a sentence becomes meaningful.

4. It Works in a Common Field of Accessibilty[2]

To the question that, if sentences of the above kind do not state any s-p that refers to f (actual or possible) for the purpose of correspondence, how can they be meaningful, one answer may be this: the apparent non-reference in some cases may be due to difference in the field of mutual accessibility of the parties concerned. But if it is believed by the hearer (or the reader, as the case may be) that the sentence in question is meaningful to all who belong to the speaker's (writer's) fraternity, the sentence is 'believed' to be meaningful.

It may be noted that a sentence is the tool of a communicative function between two persons (or their multiple) only within a common field of mutual accessibility. For example, a sentence uttered or written by a Chinese for another person of the Mandarin field of communication is a sentence. But if, on the other hand, he utters the same sentence for a Greek, it is not. For the latter it is just a bundle of sounds or signs. The vice versa is equally true. The said non-function of communicative act is because the two parties, namely, the Chinese and the Greek, do not belong to a common field of accessibility so far understanding the meaning of a sentence is concerned. Here the common field is 'common linguistic group'. This common field may be for parties falling within a scholastic fraternity (as of people studying, say, Chemistry), a group using a

[2] Compared: "The question is whether there is a fixed and universal mental world in which the word-object relation could be generalised without exception !'. D.P. Chattopadhyaya: Relativity of Language and Culture; IPQ, Vol. III, No. 2, p. 186.

common pattern of sign language, and so on. [Whether utterances or apparent scribbling falling beyond this common field can also be a sentence in some cases, is a question which we shall discuss later]

Now, let us take up a case. A Professor of chemistry complains to his morning milk-man, 'The right proportion of phospholipids and other ingredients are missing in the milk you supply'. Obviously the sentence should have sounded 'meaningless' as not stating anything that referred, for him, to some 'f' of the world that is. But how does he normally react to this? Perhaps not saying 'Sorry, Sir, you have uttered a meaningless sentence'. On the contrary, in all probability, his reply is: "Sorry, Sir, I am not competent enough to understand the meaning of the sentence. Can you please state it in simple terms !". Here he does not abandon the sentence as meaningless, but only requests for another sentence so as to reach to its meaning. Had he belonged to the Professor's fraternity of accessibility, he would have found the sentence 'meaningful'. However, this way of looking at the sentence is possible when the hearer believes that the sentence is 'meaningful', only he does not understand it.

This may be the reason why the above noted philosophical sentences may not be abandoned as 'meaningless' as a look-alike sentence like 'A square circle is blue' is. The latter is not a sentence but is treated as an utterance of words in such a way that it does not refer to a possible state of affair to which it may correspond, no question of being favourable or unfavourable. [The attribute 'blue' for geometrical figures of 'square' or 'circle' are categorically impossible to be concurrent, no question for a square-circle].

It may be noted that the words 'square', 'circle' and 'blue' of the said look-alike sentence are all 'f^{e}' s like other normal meaningful sentences. But their occurrence together as a sentence makes it 'incomprehensible' for the purpose of meaning. If, however, it is uttered with intention, as is done by the present author in this dissertation, it must have a 'meaning', though of a different kind. But in the utterance of a normal sentence 'The table is brown', the words 'The' 'table' 'is' and 'brown' make it so because the words are not only 'f^{ef}s but are uttered in such order that it states a comprehensible f, the 'brown-table'. This makes it possible to see that S refers to a 'f', and can be seen as either T or F. If the 'f' is 'Bt' (brown-table), the S is T and the sentence is meaningful. If the 'f' is Wt (white- table), the S is F and again the sentence is meaningful. In both cases the sentence facilitates the said act of correspondence on referring.

A sentence, thus, is declared 'meaningless' only when it bears words/sounds/signs that belong to a common field of accessibility of both the parties and yet the pattern 'S s-p f(T/F)' is not adhered to. If some sounds are made (words uttered or signs posted) by someone that do not fulfil the above conditions, they can be designated as 'foreign', but not 'meaningless', as was the case with the Greek and the Chinese mentioned earlier. The reason is simple. Unless the hearer (that is, the party to whom to communicate) cannot at all access the 'words' or the 'sentence' bearing them, how can he be sure that a meaningless sentence was uttered?

One who does not have any access can at best say "I do not understand what it means'. And it goes without saying, 'not knowing the meaning' of a sentence is not 'knowing it as meaningless'. So to call a sentence 'meaningless', the hearer has to ensure that he belongs to the same field of accessibility, and the uttered S is not 'foreign'.

Now, let us refer to the possible fact that, where the two parties belong to the same field, there may be two classes of utterances. One we may call UA/I where word-like utterances are accidental or involuntary; and the other UI where words are intentionally uttered to make a sentence. Word-like sounds made by a person in delirium or in a state of mental disorder are examples of the first. Such sounds are not taken as making a sentence of the latter kind.

As for (UI), words are intentionally uttered to make a sentence such that it communicates a meaning.

But there may be utterances which come under this class of the intentional ones but are meaningless. These we may call UI^1 and are distinguished from utterances under class UA/I because, here the words are intentional and are themselves of f^{fe} type. Only they are uttered in a manner such that they make a 'meaningless sentence'. "Saturday is in bed" is an instance of such sentences. That is why 'The square circle is blue' can also be designated as 'meaningless' by a student of mathematics or of English with basic access to mathematical concepts, because, the words, though individually stand for 'features of any possible f', do not fit as they occur here in the field he belongs.

The interesting feature of such sentences is that, since intentionally made, it is not absolutely meaningless. An utterance under this category states at least this fact (f), intended by the speaker, that—'This is an instance of meaningless sentence', by which it becomes 'meaningful' to a person of the same field. Sentences of this kind may, therefore, be called 'an intentional act (that is, sentence) meaningfully communicating meaninglessness'.

There is another type under this intentional utterance. Let us call it UI^2. These involves not words but some look-alike words without or along with f^{fe} words, to communicate some 'nonsense'. Lewis Carroll's 'Jabberwocky' is the best example. The first verse begins thus: "'Twas brillig and the slithy toves ....". Here except 'and' and 'the', (may be, slithy also), the other look-alike words are mere sounds without f^{ef}. But this so-called sentence is highly appreciated as 'perfect nonsense', and exactly that was the 'meaning' what the author wanted to communicate by it.

There is another interesting point about this 'unintelligibility'. An activity of a speaker/writer (in the form of a sound/sign, written words, etc.), if found 'unintelligible', does not automatically imply that it is 'meaningless'. Best examples are the archaeological finds (copper plates, stone slabs, etc.) bearing signs yet to be deciphered. Such finds are not discarded as 'meaningless'. The club-shaped images known as claviforms in the Attamira Cave of Spain, or many abstract designs or drawings in the caves are some such finds the meaning of which are yet to be deciphered, but not discarded as 'meaningless'.

Sometimes, the more any such script is unintelligible, the more it is valued as priceless, provided that is genuine. In a high class comedy play of Tagore (Baikunther Khata), a crazy Bengali character of the play, who is mad to find an un-deciphered pre-historic script, comes across an account book written in Mandarin by a shoe-maker of China Bazar of Calcutta, brought to him as an ancient script. He finds it absolutely unintelligible and goes ecstatic to exclaim: "*kii chomotkar, kicchu bojha jaye na*" ('How amazing, nothing of it is intelligible'). Here, the fun of the cheating act apart, the sentence uttered by him bears this implicit truth that 'if genuine, the unintelligible may be immensely meaningful'.

5. 'Meaning' is Not Limited to 'Unity' of Acquaintance

Awareness from acquaintance means having a direct knowledge. This may be of an object based on sense-contact such that each of the different data of the object is sensed by the respective sense organ. To quote Russell: "We shall say that we have acquaintance with anything of we are directly aware, without the intermediary of any process of inference… ".[3] Thus, according to him, one is acquainted with, say, a table, means he is directly acquainted with its colour, shape, hardness, smoothness, etc. In other words, the awareness or communication caused by a sentence 'The table is brown' is based on direct contact of the sense organ. For awareness of such facts, it is the direct acquaintance of the person concerned. For communicating the same to a hearer, it is required for both. (Without this sense contact common field, this awareness will not be communicated to the hearer in the intended manner).

However, when one utters a sentence 'Greatness lies in unity in diversity', the awareness caused to him by it is not based on his sense-contact as above. But the direct acquaintance required here is with

[3]B. Russell: The Problems of Philosophy, 1973, p. 25.

the universals used in the sentence. And according to Russell, this 'becoming aware of the universals' is called 'conceiving' and what the person is aware of is called a concept. The same acquaintance is also required for the hearer to get the meaning of such sentences.

Now, in respect of meaning of a sentence referring to states of affair of the world, if we go by such direct acquaintance with respective data of a thing, making the 'fact' of reference, then perhaps no 'referring' of the S of a sentence would have at all been possible, and, therefore, no meaning of it. Let us take a few examples to see why it is so, taking A for the speaker and B for the hearer.

Case No. 1: *A and B are both directly in contact with the object.*

The situation is such that A is standing on that side of a table which faces sufficient sunlight. He must be directly in contact with the colour-data of the table which is 'usual brown colour'. He utters a sentence 'The table is brown" by which he is supposed to refer to 'a-usual-brown-coloured-table'. Let us call this M^1. Now, B is standing on the opposite side, that is, the side that faces the less lighted, rather darker, side of the table. To him the sentence is 'perfectly meaningful' as T, satisfying required correspondence condition. But in all probability, the meaning B accesses would be a 'dark-brown-coloured- table' (M^2), because for him only that colour could have been directly contacted by his eyes. But B accesses the sentence 'The table is brown' intended by A to be M^1 as meaningfully stating a S as T, whereas he should have accessed it meaningful only as F. This requires us to concede that, for the sake of meaning of a sentence, direct acquaintance may not be strictly adhered to:

Case No. 2: *B has no acquaintance.*

A, a resident of Agartala, says: "Ujjayanta Palace is at the centre of Agartala". B never visited the city, but heard of it. He gets the meaning without personal acquaintance with the f referred to. Here he takes the f on the basis of 'what it should be', *taking* the speaker a truthful one.

Case No. 3: *Neither A nor B in definite contact.*

In a place having insufficient light for visual perception, A looks at something at a distance and utters "Is that a man or a post?" Here the sentence states 'Here is a f about which nothing can be said with certainty', and B very well gets the meaning having referred to that f not because of acquaintance, but rather of the absence of it. Indeed, here the S of the sentence refers to a situation.

Thus we find that so far meaning of a sentence is concerned, we cannot be limited to our having direct acquaintance with the referred object that is the state of affairs. If we do so, the intention of the speaker and the access of the hearer shall be different, leading to failure of the purpose of the whole exercise. But we frequently utter sentences of the above kind.

What then is the fate of such a sentence? Is it a futile exercise to deliver a meaning? Obviously not, for, a hearer does have access to the meaning of a sentence like 'The table is brown' as T, however based on direct acquaintance with different states. How this is possible, we shall come to that after we discuss the meaning of sentences involving universal concepts.

Case No. 4: *A concept rather than a state of the affair is referred to.*

A says to B: "Unity in diversity is the essence of Indianness". Here what A intends to refer to is not a state of affair of the world like a table which we can be acquainted with. But the concepts used in the sentence to make a S which states a 'state' of the form, to use Russell's phrase, 'a so-and-so' or 'the so-and-so', as the case may be, to mean not an 'object-f' but a 'concept-f'. And B accesses the meaning of the sentence without any difficulty because concepts can stand the test of correspondence in a completely different plain, namely, the common field of conceptuality.

The term 'conceptually common field' may sound as ambitious an idea as 'meeting of two parallel lines at infinity'. No body 'knows' what exactly is infinity and what happens to parallel lines there. But we 'take' it as a 'mathematical' state of affair. Mathematics is an abstract science, based on rationality of relation between concepts. Similarly a sentence uttered by A using concepts can create in the mind of B a sort of rationality of relations of the 'same', which works as following the pattern 'S s-p f(T/F)' and produces meaning.

It may be noticed that about the utterance conforming to the pattern of meaning in the above we have said 'same', but with reservations. Because, concepts are mental and no two minds can be exactly identically operative. Referring to a concept as f varies with how much the minds of A and B are equipped to access the said concept backed by their experience, capacity to apply mind, and so on. And as the concepts may vary, the rationality of their relation must also be of different kind. But, in spite of this individual differences, the sentence 'Unity in ...etc.', uttered by A is meaningfully communicated to B as T or as F, as the case may be, and not treated as 'foreign'.

This also shows that, whether we go by direct acquaintance or by concepts, there is always an element of 'believed agreement' between A and B to belong to a common field of accessibility, the prime basis of meaningful communication.

[This 'compromise' aspect of meaning is discussed in Chapter 'Meaning, Concept and Compromise' of this book.]

6. The Law of Cause and Effect Working in its Passage to Meaning

Referring to the preceding section, it may be asked: how can a nonsense 'sentence', or a sentence that is 'foreign', can be meaningful without their competence for correspondence for T/F? In this context, it may be said that the most striking fact about a sentence is that we never say anything intentionally that is 'nonsense' (that is, without anything to convey) or something that we know as 'false'. About the first, we have already discussed in the previous section. About the second, we may recall that, when we utter a sentence to state some S, we do so only to 'see' that it refers favourably to exactly the same f that was intended. One cannot intentionally utter a sentence to state something as 'is' to mean 'is not' (that is, stating 's is p' intending 's is not p') unless he so intends with a definite purpose (may be, to mislead, to cheat, or with such other intentions). So, speaking of a normally uttered sentence, when one utters it, he states a S (s is p or s is not-p) that is only T, because that is the demand of the Law of Cause and Effect. It is this way that Nature works with the law in every field including human field.[4]

So it comes to saying that, a sentence as a tool of communication has always to communicate something that is true. In other words, under natural conditions of language at work (involving uttering - hearing, writing-reading, etc.), we do not make a sentence to state the S to turn false. How this natural condition works, may be stated as follows.

In uttering a sentence for communication, there is produced the **cause** by coming together of the following natural happenings:

> 'The speaker's awareness(s is p), his intention to communicate the same to the hearer, right words chosen in uttering the sentence to state the same (s is p)'.

The effect that follows in the hearer's mind:

> 'The-meaning (s is p)'. That means, what the sentence states is 'True'. If, however, for some reasons, which too is natural, it turns F, it can be explained within the law of cause-and-effect. Before we do that, it may be noted that, the F of the S of the sentence is again 'awareness' by another sentence that states S^2 meaning 's-is-not-p' and follows the same course of cause-effect in affecting the same reception in the hearer.

At times, as we have said, the S turns F. Therefore it may be asked, if the whole activity is a natural process involving man, then

---

4 "...in the universe everything is in a chain process of cause-effect or action–reaction affair, be it in the physical field, in the biological field, or in the human field". Author's: TRUTH a Work of Nature in Man. Allied Pub. New Delhi, p. 67.

why in some cases nature behaves so 'unnaturally' that it does not follow its own law of 'same cause to lead to same effect' in the case of the referring act of a sentence? We have seen instead, there are cases of sentences the S stated by which, following nature's law of uniformity, should have stated only T, but turns F. Is it because man's thought and 'intention' (behind the sentence) do not come under Nature's law like other things of nature? It is not so. Though it appears to be 'un-natural', such cases of non-abiding by cause-effect law of Nature are also within the working process of the Law of Nature.

It is true that Nature works in such a rigid law-bound pattern that, under similar conditions, the effect of a cause is always predictable. But in its working, Nature itself takes leave of its own rigidity. For example, the reproductive process in the bio-world requires, as law, a sort of fertilisation. But in the case of 'Parthenogenesis', nature refutes its own law of cause-effect such that, it is born of Parthenogenesis. This is commonly known as virgin birth, which is a form of reproduction without fertilisation or the fusion of gametes.

Similar 'unnatural' behaviour of Nature in respect of passage from cause to its effect can be cited from the more rigid world of Physics too. For example, we learn from the physicist that if a proton is bombarded into nucleus, what is ejected should always be a proton by the law of 'same cause same effect', but sometimes it is a neutron.[5]

If, therefore, a sentence states something that is false when it was supposed to state only T, it does not behave un-naturally. A sentence 'always' states a S that is 'true'. An intentional sentence that states a lie, a puzzle, or the like, though performs a different function, comes under the same pattern of always stating a S that is T. The difference it bears is that it 'favourably' refers to the f that is 'a different kind of state of the affair'. For example, 'a misrepresented state of the affair'

[5] Evans R.D.: The Atomic Nucleus, McGraw-Hill, pp. 350–51.

is the *intended* fact of the speaker telling a lie, where his intention is 'amusing the audience by baffling'. This is the intended situation or fact of uttering a puzzle.

In short, therefore, it may be said, in spite of difference in kind, sentences uttered with intention follow the same *natural law* of 'a cause leading to its effect' in the human field as it follows in other fields of it. And therefore, to question the effect of (that is a fact referred by) a sentence as 'whether it is the same f that the S refers to', (that is, whether the S is true), shall be the same as questioning, say, whether the effect 'tremor of a bursting cracker' caused by the bursting of a cracker is truly so produced or not.[6]

And, this cause-effect chain relation between a fact, a sentence, and its meaning referring to that fact, perhaps, is 'the' reason why one, uttering a sentence to another's detriment, cannot disown it by just saying: 'What's in a sentence'.

We may now go for the concluding remarks:

1. An intentional sentence is always meaningful both to the person who makes it for his awareness and to the person/persons whom he wants to communicate the awareness by it.
2. A meaningful sentence is so because it refers to a fact or a state of the affair of the world.
3. The referred fact is a 'situation of the world that is' such that the f can be without having any physical occurrence.
4. Such reference, therefore, requires a conceptual agreement.
5. The birth of a sentence in human field is naturally caused by some f which the sentence refers to in return. It, therefore, follows that the natural law of cause and effect ensures that it refers to a 'fact that has caused it'. This also ensures that no sentence is born to state some fact 'falsely', as no smoke

[6] A study on the topic can be found in the author's "Truth a work of Nature in Man"; Allied Publishers. New Delhi. Chapter 3.

'occurs' (is affected) to indicate fire 'behind' (causing the smoke) falsely. That would go against the law of causation.

6. That some s-p stated by a sentence S is F does not invalidate No. 5 above, but shows that in the case of this human activity too Nature reveals variations, though, again, within its law.

Meaning, Concept and Compromise[1]

1. The 'Non-factual' Interpretation of Sentence for Meaning

In the previous chapter we have said that, what a sentence refers to as a fact is not an 'object of the world', but 'a state of the affair' that, along with others, make 'the world that is' for man. The said contention suggests that the fact is a 'situation rather than an object' that man 'accepts' as 'all that makes the world for him for all practical and reasonable purpose'. In this connection, we would mention the views of Russell and Wittgenstein, as expressed in the following, to extend this contention to its logical conclusion.

Russell in one of his Lectures says: "…when I speak of a fact I do not mean a particular existing thing, such as Socrates, or the rain or the sun. Socrates himself does not render any statement true or false.....What I call a fact is the sort of thing that is expressed by a whole sentence."[2] And Wittgenstein's Tractatus says: "We use the perceptible sign of a proposition (spoken or written, etc.) as a projection of a possible situation. (T.3.11). I call the sign with which we express a thought a propositional sign. And a proposition is a propositional sign in its projective relation to the world. (T.3.12). What constitute a propositional sign is that in it its elements (the words) stand in a determinate relation to one another. A propositional sign is a fact (T.3.14)."

What the two above contentions suggest, to state in simpler terms, is that the referred 'fact' that makes a sentence meaningful, on the basis of the stated proposition, forms a part of what 'we find

[1] A revised version of an Article of the same title published in Indian Philosophical Quarterly, Vol. 35, No. 1–4, Jan.–Dec., 2008.

[2] B. Russell: Lectures collected in 'The Philosophy of Logical Atomism', 1972, p. 7.

as our only possible world'. In other words, the referred fact of a sentence is not a material thing but a *situation conceptually found possible.* However, before we go on to deliberate on this, let us refer to a few schools of philosophy that advocate a 'non-mental' model that explains how and what a sentence means.

According to the Indian Grammarian school of Bhartrhari, which advocates that *Sabda Brahman* is the only Real, the world is made not of 'objects' or elements of matter, mind, etc., but of *Sabda* or 'words' including their sentential occurrences. These words, sentences, etc., coming up in course of interaction between individuals are, says Bhartrihari, not creation of the cognitive act in the traditional sense, but the 'evolves' of *Sabda* within the action-reaction frame work of that Ultimate Reality.[3]

So, regarding meaning of a verbal occurrence, the view of this school may be stated as follows: what A utters to B is not an individual's verbal exercise carrying some awareness, sensation, etc., of his own intended to be understood by the latter, but an occurrence within the system of *Sabda,* the ultimate frame of Reality. Against this contention, the view that upholds the individual role in this matter to mean that, a man understands the meaning of a sentence as he individually thinks it to be, in fact suggests an unworkable hypothesis of 'private language'. Wittgenstein discarded such a hypothesis[4] on the simple ground that a language understandable by only a single individual is incoherent. In 'Philosophical Investigations' he writes "The meaning of a word is not the experience one has in hearing or saying it, and the sense of a sentence is not a complex of such experiences." (Sec VI, Part II)

The *Sabda* theory holds that, there cannot be any idea or concept that is meant by someone by uttering a sentence that goes by any subjective intention. On the contrary, the sentence, to be meaningful, must comply with the self-regulated system of its

---

[3] Battacharya B.P.: A Study in Languages and Meaning: 'The Relation of Words with their Meanings'.

[4] Engg. Translation: Amethe Smeaton, Open Court. Chicago.

occurrence free from any subjective element. Therefore, in a sentence that is uttered, the object of its reference cannot be anything that is rooted in the speaker's personal intention, that is, mind. Because, an object of reference is a non-entity unless it has a manifestation in *Sabda* or, what is commonly called, *Language.* In other words, when a sentence is uttered, no 'special' effort is required to reach on to its meaning, because, sentences can occur within the world of *Sabda* only with their self-manifested reality, that is, their meaning.

But if the *Sabda* – world were sufficient to make an expression with definitive meaning of it, and there were nothing to consider for its definiteness outside the *Sabda* – world, then, let us mention only one instance to show its inadequacy and that is the case of an expression in *samsaya* or doubt where one, looking at something standing at a distance, utters "Is that a post or a man?" Obviously, the significance of the expression remains 'unattainable' because the speaker and the hearer have to depend, for its significance, on what falls outside the so defined language world.

Rudolf Carnap, writing about his 'Languages As Calculi' in 'The Logical Syntax of Language'[5] thought of a possible system of concepts, a language with the help of which the results of logical analysis of the concepts in use could be exactly determined. He writes: "The rules of calculus determines, in the first place, the conditions under which an expression can be said to belong to a certain category of expressions." And, "An expression of this language is called a sentence when it consists, in such and such a way, of symbols of such and such a kind, occurring in such and such an order." The language thus devised could function without the participation of individual or collective experiences of facts of the world harboured in one's mind.

But the language he devised was full of complex artificial formulae which, considered from the point of its use in ordinary life,

[5] B. Russell: Mr. Strawson on Referring. Classics of Analytical Philosophy. Ammerman, N.Y. 1965, p. 338.

failed to provide the very basic requirement namely, understanding a proposition made by a sentence about 'the material world'. For him, the words are symbols in a particular order or relation (making it logically possible) to make a sentence meaningful as either analytic or contradictory.

For example, a proposition states that there is a fact of the world, x, taken up to 3 positions, and x is red. Translated into logical form it will be:

1. There is an x in 3 positions such that x is red in all 3 of them.

   Or. 2. Of the 3 positions of x, at least in one of them it is red.

The former is known as universal proposition, the latter, an existential proposition. Now, if the two are put into their respective logical syntax, they will be:

1. For all x, x is 'Red(0). Red(1). Red (2). Red (3)' [the dots(.) standing for 'and']. And
2. For existential x, x is 'Red(0)V Red (1) V Red (2) V Red (3)' [symbol V standing for 'or').

Now, Carnap says, if we can translate all sentences of a language in their logical syntax, then truth/falsity (as analytic/contradictory) of any of them could be logically derived from propositions related to it as 'premise'. Our doing with the language world is wholly governed by the rules of logic.

But, the question what such a contention faces is, however the unshakable truth of a logical proposition is derived independently of the truth of x in reality, at the end of the day does not such truth depend on the favourable or unfavourable reference of x to the intended fact of the world? In other words, how to get to the meaning of the sentence stating 'x is red' which refers simply to its worldly positions as 'this and this' .... or 'this or this'...? Carnap calls them 'synthetic sentences' which are 'not resoluble'. In his words, "... they are neither demonstrable nor refutable". Further he said, 'A synthetic sentence is sometimes true- namely, when certain facts exist- and sometimes false...'. And that they are decided by such effort that is not covered by his logic, he himself agreed to that. In Theorem 14.4. He says, "..the question of *logical* congruence of meaning has no connection with that of the agreement of conceptions and the like. The latter is a question of psychological nature and must therefore be decided by empirical and psychological investigation."

The only question, therefore, remains to be answered: Do we have a meaningful world without these sentences of logical syntax? Russell, in outlining a programme for a logical framework of the world in propositions, says:" In accordance with the sort of realistic bias that I should put into all study of metaphysics, I should always wish to be engaged in the investigations of some actual fact or set of facts and it seems to me that that is so in logic...different sorts of facts, different *logical* sorts of facts, that there are in the world".

Thus, in respect of meaning of a sentence referring to a fact of the world, so far the 'speaker-hearer unity' is deemed essential, what is basically required is an active role of both the speaker and the hearer. No other rule, logical or whatever, can govern it.

Wittgenstein calls this participation (of speaker-hearer) 'Language Game', meaning a social model of life in which words are used as 'construction material' (where in a construction work the mason asks for, say, a 'slab' and his assistant hands it over to him without difficulty). According to him, 'Meaning just is use', which is governed by a *social bond of communication* where the speaker intends to deliver something through his utterance of words, sentences, etc. (not logical symbols anyway) and the hearer receives that in the same form within a 'unity framework'. This implies that, in the absence of any two of the preconditions, namely, the intention to deliver and the affected reception in the intended sense respectively, there cannot be any meaning of the word 'slab', mentioned above.

2. The Speaker-hearer Participation

Thus, it may be said that, the two preconditions, namely, the role of intention of one to convey and reception by another forming two parties in this process of communication become more important than anything else. This will be evident from a possible case as described below.

Let us consider a case where a set of word-like signs somehow comes up on a sheet of paper by an unmindful scribbler behind which there was no intention of saying something. It may be that the scribbling so created look like a sentence conveying some meaning. Yet the scribbler is not held responsible for the meaning conveyed by 'it', and hence, it should be treated as 'outside the scope of meaning (of a sentence)'.

There may also be another case where the scribbling is done wilfully, but without any intention or plan to communicate anything. For example, we can think of a hypothetical case where a primitive man at the time when language was not discovered started scratching on the wall of a cave for his amusement. Incidentally the scratches discovered by a later researcher are found resembling some words which, taken for a sentence, 'communicate' some meaning. But, certainly, he is not to consider the so-called words for a sentence by someone and for someone. They would rather be more reasonably treated as 'a collection of physical objects' just like we treat a collection of pebbles found inside a cave.

Now, sometimes it is discovered (by researchers) that the said scratches are found together in such a manner that they may be taken for a 'sentence' conveying 'some meaning'. Should we ignore them as pieces of 'physical objects' as described in the previous paragraph, or call it a 'sentence' of some sort? The answer shall be: 'It depends'. Here the two basic requirements noted earlier are to be taken into consideration before rejecting them or taking them for making a sentence to communicate some meaning. Firstly, the researcher must here be the 'receiver party in agreement' the sense, he finds them to form a S (sentence) conveying some meaning. And, secondly, he believes that there was someone whose intention was to convey that particular meaning to the prospective 'reader'.

In fact, that is the reason why many of the scribbling found in caves, on rocks and mountain walls, etc., are not summarily ignored as 'meaningless' act of 'mindless limb movement' of the homo sapiens of that period. Rather the truth is that, hundreds of such scribbling have been deciphered through ages by archaeologists and researchers of calligraphy that 'speak' lots about those ancient people. And that happened only because such discoveries complied with the two requirements stated above, and were supported by lots of other scientific tests, logically woven, with regard to establishing the 'intention' part of the 'writer' (scribbler) on the one hand and the ground for receiving those in their intended meaning by the 'reader' (the researcher), on the other.

3. 'Meaning' is a 'Mental Process of Participation'

We come back to our initial contention that meaning in communication depends on a mental process involving the speaker and the hearer, a process that unites the two parties on the meaning conveyed and received respectively, through a sentence uttered or an expression of any other form made for the purpose. In other words, a sentence S is meaningful because of an active participation both by the speaker and the hearer as the intending and the receiving partners.

There may, however, be exceptional situations where an utterance is made by someone with intention to communicate and there is a hearer to receive it, but the utterance is made in such form or syntax that it conveys practically nothing. For example, to borrow from Russell's 'Mr. Strawson on Referring', we can think of a situation where the master of a house accuses his maidservant of thieving, and she replies "I ain't never done no harm to no one". Her utterance, it is presumed, has an honest intention to convey that she has always been a virtuous lady, never harming anybody, as it is in this case too. But the way she utters, says Russell, "...according to the rules of syntax which Mr. Strawson would adopt... what she said should have meant: 'there was at least one moment when I was injuring the whole human race.' Mr. Strawson would not have supposed that this was what she meant to assert...".

This contention of Russell implies that, the meaning conveyed by the utterance should have been received not by the utterance as such but along with other considerations based on the concept of the virtuous character of the lady in the receiver's mind. In other words, meaning of a sentence can occur between a speaker and a hearer just on the strength of the utterance alone, but it must be supported by an 'active participation' of both. Thus, instead of going through a mechanical process involving the passive role that a speaker-hearer complex is supposed to have so far meaning of a sentence is concerned, what this 'active participation' could be? Before we go for our view in this respect, let us refer to Russell's for a while in this regard.

In his theory of 'Description' [appearing as 'On Denoting' (Mind, Vol. XIV, 1905) and later further developed in 'Introduction to Mathematical Philosophy', 1919] he says that, a sentence uttered by someone using a description like 'a so and so' or 'the so and so' can be significant to the hearer even if it does not specifically refer to anything. About the first, which according to him is an indefinite description, he says: when one says 'I met a man', he does not really assert that he met Peter or Jones or, for that matter, any such specific person, though may be he actually met Jones. But the sentence 'I met a man' remains significant to the hearer irrespective of any specific person referred to by the description 'a man'. He in fact believes that, not only no Jones, but no actual man enters into this statement. He further extends this to say that "Indeed the statement would remain significant, though it could not be possibly true, even if there were no man at all." Thus, according to him, "'I met a unicorn' or 'I met a sea-serpent' is a perfectly significant assertion, if we knew what it would be to be a unicorn or a sea-serpent, i.e. what is the definition of these fabulous monsters."

And to know the definition of a term is to know that it stands for such and such, that is, to have a concept about it. That is why, we may say, Russell says "Thus it is only what we may call the *concept* that enters into the proposition, it is clear that this proposition ('I met a unicorn') rightly analysed, does not contain a constituent 'a unicorn', though it does contain the concept 'unicorn'.[B. Russell: *Descriptions.* Ammerman's 'Classics of Analytic Philosophy', p. 16.]

4. Conceptual Unity: How Far Achievable

Now, what we shall see in the following is that, the word 'concept' used by Russell has not been amply analysed and that if it were so analysed, it would have raised a few questions regarding one most important point, namely, what is the nature of the two parties involved in accomplishing access to the said concept. We shall see that the word 'concept' is a very 'notorious' customer in the process of communication between the speaker and the hearer. It involves several elements including a person's mental structure and his world of experience which practically may make the understanding of statements like 'I met a man', 'I have a pain', or 'I achieved a heavenly vision' more confusing, rather enigmatic, than making it significant. Let us see how.

Firstly, a concept X is not a fundamental element of thought process such that it could be assumed to have identically occurred in the mind of every rational being. It, on the contrary, is a mental state that is formed by the respective mind on the basis of experiences computed with mental traits of emotion, sentiment, attitude, and so on. And as each man's experiences, his emotions, attitude, etc. are uniquely his own, it is hardly possible that A and B can share X exactly in the same way. And, therefore, this *sharing the concept in the same shape* in an act of communication remains inadmissible.

Secondly, there may be cases where A has a concept X but B does not have that concept at all, no question of identical occurrence to the two minds. Let us take the third example above in support of this. Suppose A is a person of such religious bend of mind that he rigorously practices the direct vision method of accessing what he believes as 'heavenly truths'. One day he exclaims in excitement to B: 'Look! I achieved a heavenly vision!' B is a person who has no religious or spiritual leaning whatsoever. Now, irrespective of whether what A uttered was true or false, can we expect that B will be in a position to share the expression 'a heavenly vision', for the purpose of meaning, to find whether it was true or false? Certainly that is ruled out, for he does not know what 'a heavenly vision' at all is. In fact, this is what exactly happened in a case reported by 'The Times Of India' (October 15, 2009), where a god man of a Madhya Pradesh temple of India immolated himself in front of scores of people including senior police officials, saying, he was taking a '*Samaadhi*' (a merger with godliness). Everybody watched the event in awe not knowing how to react to his utterance along with his actions, for, obviously, nobody present there had any concept of 'taking a *samaadhi*' so that they could stop him (from committing a crime for something that was false) or applaud him (for his heavenly act).

This is a unique, rather a very unusual, case where sharing on the basis of concept is found totally impossible. But accessibility or sharing is no better even in more common utterances. Let us consider the S 'I have a pain'. Suppose A says to B: 'I have a chest pain'. The description 'a chest pain' refers to a concept relating to his thought of the severe pain totally occupying his body and mind at that moment. Let us call this pain, P1. Now, B or, anyone for that matter, to whom the sentence is uttered to communicate the state of pain, may be a person who never had any chest pain or any kind of similar pain. But B had seen one of his dearest ones die of heart attack, complaining chest pain. He remembers that painful incident at the instance of chest pain. Let us call this memory (concept?) of pain of his as a helpless onlooker, P2. Now, can we expect that B will be accessing the meaning of the description 'a chest pain' with the concept P1and not P2? It may be that, B says to A with genuine sorry feeling that 'I feel so bad for the pain you are having'. But surely so saying, he would be referring to his concept of 'chest pain', namely, $P^{2,}$ and not P^1 of A. That means, what is usually taken for 'sharing' (or having conceptual unity), is only a matter of 'make belief' in achieving so.

This non-unity factor cannot be ruled out in the cases of sentences using Russell's 'indefinite' and 'definite' descriptions. For example, when a Clergyman, using an indefinite description, refers to an incident of meeting a poor man saying 'I met a man', the man, whoever he was, was for him 'a son of God'. But the person hearing the utterance, being an ordinary man of all likely worldly characteristics, will take the sentence as meaning 'The Clergyman met just another person like him'.

Similarly, in the case of the use of definite descriptions, the sentence 'Scott is the author of Waverly' uttered by A, a litterateur, is likely to convey his intention of naming a literary great as the person authoring Waverly. Russell said, it would mean three things, namely, 1. Scott is a person. 2. Waverly is a literary creation authored by someone. And 3. Scott authored Waverly. These are the minimum information which the hearer B's mental world must accommodate to understand the meaning of the sentence of this definite description kind. But B may be a fish trader of the Sunderbans of no acquaintance whatsoever with literature. He only knew that the word 'authoring' means 'inventing a new plan (which is also an accepted meaning of the word)'. So he as a fish trader thought the speaker was referring to a new method of fishing and therefore the meaning of the sentence he would access would more likely be, "There was a person such and such who did some invention regarding fishing method of the name 'Waverly'". Surely a situation like that would be most unwanted. But this cannot be helped unless there is 'conceptual unity' between the speaker and the hearer, and the more we proceed, the more we shall find that, that is most unlikely to happen.

Let us take another example where the meaning of a sentence with definite description cannot be ordinarily accessed unless the 'time' of occurrence is mentioned. The sentence beginning with 'The King of France…', (1) if stated as of today, is meaningless for, whatever is said about 'the king', today there is no king of France at all; (2) if stated to refer to the time of Louis XIV, then whatever stated about him would be meaningful in the sense of being either true or false. But the question is, would a sentence like this shall be meaningful as 'commonly shared' (by the speaker and the hearer) just by mention of the time of occurrence? Perhaps not, for the simple reason that may be one of the two or even both may lack any knowledge of history. Therefore, reference of time would not be of any help in accessing a situation referred by the sentence. In other words, there are always more than one reasons why a speaker and a hearer do not share a common frame of mind towards achieving the unity of concept.

We shall, now, try to examine what Mr. Strawson believed about what could enable the hearer to identify to what is being talked about by the speaker in a sentence. In 'On Referring', he says: "In securing this result, the context of utterance is of an importance which it is almost impossible to exaggerate..." And by 'context' he means "at least, the time, the place, the situation, the identity of the speaker, the subjects which form the immediate focus of interest, and the personal histories of both the speaker and those he is addressing." (p. 329).

Now, this 'contextual identity', if we may so call it, implies that the two parties in question stick to one common subject of focus in course of the communicative act. But as soon as we refer to the world of experience and the social situational history of each, this identification becomes hardly possible. Let us take an example to show how it differs in the actual world.

A poor daily wage earner of the third world country knows that earning sufficient money is not possible for a lone earner in a family. So, as we often gather, there are stories in abundance where the husband prays that his wife gives birth to as many children as possible without thinking about how they would survive. His situation and the socio-economic background frames a mind-set in him which thinks 'to have more children is to have the grace of God'. Now, how a social activist, who is working tirelessly in that particular country to educate people to undertake strict birth control programme for the good of the family and of his country, would react to such a claim that 'a larger fleet of children' means 'a grace of God'? He would certainly call it a social ignorance, rather than true or false. And that the right meaning of the said expression did not reach the poor man is only because his thinking of social need did not match that of the activist or of people of similar belief.

Here the meaning of an expression differs so clearly because of very clear situational difference. This cannot be ruled out also in cases where we believe to have obtained apparent unity. And this may happen due, at least, to difference of personal interest involved in the expression. Let us take the example of two persons, A and B. The former is an art lover and appreciates heritage paintings for their high artistic value. B is a trader of heritage painting pieces. The two meet in an exhibition of heritage collections. A says to B: 'This exhibition has a valuable collection'. B replies: 'Yes, it has a valuable collection'. Here we find that both A and B are using the same phrase and refer to the 'same fact', namely, 'the value of collection (of art pieces)', and that a sort of 'identity' occurs between them. But we can very well imagine that while A must have meant by the phrase 'a valuable collection' the high artistic value of the paintings, for B it was more likely that he referred to the trading value of such heritage paintings. Here the communication is not accomplished on the basis of real unity of concept, but only on a 'presumed unity'.

5. Meaning as 'Compromise'

We may now go on to state our view. We have seen that 'meaning' of a sentence as intended by the speaker and received by the hearer requires a sort of union as the end-product of the effort. But since practical factors are not conducive to such union, it can be thought of only as a 'make-belief' of an occurrence of identity taking place in it. We may call it a sort of 'compromise' to reach that conceptual unity. Even though no two persons can have identical conceptual approach, A's and B's approach interacts with each other as a 'compromise activity'. When the hearer believes that he is sharing the concept conveyed by the utterance of the speaker (which in fact he is not), and also makes the speaker believe that he is actually doing it, there actually occurs a compromising act in the whole affair. It is, we may say, of the form of '*not exactly getting the meaning and yet, on the one hand, giving the belief to himself that he got it, and giving the same belief, on the other, to the speaker that, he got it*'.

In other words, what goes on in the name of communication of some meaning by utterance and reception of a sentence is a pseudo-communication. It occurs on the basis of some make belief, an intellectual and/or emotional compromise that it has so occurred. The speaker A cannot reasonably believe that the conveyed meaning through the sentence he utters shall be perfectly accessed by the hearer B. Similarly, B cannot reasonably believe that he has perfectly got into the concept intended by A. Yet both A and B go for a 'belief' that they have successfully done the job. This I call the 'make-belief' between them. This make-belief, we may say, is the result of the demand of their human nature to remain happy with a workable compromise for life.

The 'demand', so to say, for such compromise as human beings may be demonstrated as follows. Let us take the case of A stating groaningly' I have a pain', where it is more likely that he wanted to convey to B the harrowing state he was passing through at that moment. But B must miss that state of feeling because of his past history of no pain in life. Yet, if we look at B's reaction to A, we find, almost invariably that he deeply sympathises with him saying 'Oh ! I feel so bad that you are in this kind of pain ! ", or something like that. This he does not because he could access the meaning of the S, namely, the pain (because that is not possible for him for he personally had no concept of pain).But practically he does it because that was the 'required' mode of verbal response to such communication and also because that is the 'social etiquette'. While the former is a mechanical action–reaction process in the event of the particular physical occurrence against some particular kinds of sound (here those created by the utterance of the said words) like any other physical occurrence in the world, the latter is a compromising act of the individual facilitating the former to happen. Every social being is believed to indulge in forms of such reactions under social models such that the world keeps going. Incidentally, the first is the *initiator* of the second. Here the physical occurrence of the expression 'pain' (uttering the word in a particular gesture of the body and/or face) works as a catalyst that initiates the required workable sharing of the '**concept pain**' by the two minds involved.

The above instance is a case of emotional solidarity for which everybody would appreciate B to have rightly exhibited. But it remains a fact that for any experience X by A to be communicated to B, what B receives in each case is either Y or Z or.... It may be, also have the name X, but without knowing that X, i.e. what is *the meaning* that A wanted to convey to him by the sentence. Such X is just a 'working name' to help the process of interaction under social consensus. Strawson mentioned, the use of the article 'the' used by the speaker before a word, such as 'the table', very easily works for a unity of conception so intended. Here, says Strawson,".. 'the' shows, but does not state, that we are, or intend to be referring, to one particular individual..." He said so perhaps for this simple reason that it depended on several conditions. He said: '... a matter to be determined from context, time, place, and any other features of the utterance."

What all these factors in the referring and understanding act of a sentence indicate is nothing but this important fact that meaning of a sentence is a kind of 'agreement reached on the basis of several factors working on the speaker and the hearer at the time of communication, both physical and mental.' (In Strawson's words:

'The general moral of all these is that communication is much less a matter of explicit or disguised assertion than logicians used to suppose.')

What we take out of these observations is that they reiterate our contention, namely, that what goes on in the name of 'telling something' and 'receiving the same thing' is sheer conventional verbal exercise displaying a make-belief of unity, a pseudo communication between a speaker and a hearer. This is what we called 'compromise' with the situation of not fulfilling the required conditions of real unity, a compromise that occurs for several reasons: social, intellectual, emotional, situational, and so on.

This 'union of the concept of the referred object' is not just a linguistic feature as many have thought, but a demand of Nature pervading everything including our social bond for working together. It is the demand of our existence which does not allow individuals to roam about in strictly private worlds like that of Crusoe. Interaction between individuals is the basic need of survival. So, however impossible such interaction in the real sense might appear, from love-making to war-cry, from the share market analysis to spiritual guidance, the world goes on with the belief that the intended meaning in each case is being accessed. If this accessing takes the route of logical conclusiveness, then perhaps no Adams would have responded Eves and therefore no human race and no need for any communicative act either.

That this willingness for conceptual union is the basis of all communication becomes also evident if we look at cases where it does not exist. Gandhi's acts expressing love for all men was not 'understood' by the then Rulers of South Africa (for which they rained hostility on him instead of responding with befitting gesture), not because they could not 'access' the meaning of the word 'love' but because they were unwilling to share the meaning of it with that non-white speaker.

Now, when we say that conceptual unity for meaning is not practically possible and that the unity thus appearing to have reached is nothing but a sort of compromise between the speaker and the hearer, this is not to make an unconditional statement. Statements of Logic and Mathematics and of those based on fundamental laws of thought are perfectly communicable on the basis of unity of thought, because, they appeal only to reason in exclusion of any personal elements (or 'features' as thought of by Strawson, mentioned above). But, since, they differ from utterance of sentences made by a speaker to communicate some meaning to a hearer in the ordinary sense in having a well-defined realm of thought, the meaning and significance of such statements of Logic and Mathematics, or similar other fundamental realm of knowledge call for a separate study beyond the present deliberation.

The Linguists and the Indian Grammarians*

ABSTRACT: The Linguistic Philosophy, admittedly initiated by Wittgenstein, is, in a sense, a revolutionary trend in this field of human research since it claims itself to be euthanasia of traditional philosophy. According to it, the first (and also the last) truth for man for all practical purpose is that 'the world is that is the case'. Traditional philosophers tried to go beyond it posing questions like, 'what is the ultimate reality of the universe', 'what is the truth of appearance and reality', or 'what is the possibility or impossibility of independent object', and so on which, according to them, are meaningless on two counts. Firstly, none of them could provide a conclusive answer to such questions. Secondly, and more importantly, all questions so posed and all attempted answers are possible only in and through language that man uses. Therefore, language, more particularly the use of language by man is the only thing philosophy can be concerned with.

Indian philosophy, on the other hand, is famous for its spiritual search for the transcendental reality behind this world. According to one school, the reality is One, and that the non-dual Supreme Consciousness or Brahman, being indeterminate in nature, assumes determinate worldly forms to us due to avidyaa, etc. According to another, the ultimate objectivity of the world is made of subtle independent padaarthas or categories behind all worldly forms, and so on. Also there were schools which, on the basis of their knowledge believed that only that world that is perceived is real.

But none of these schools is comparable to that of the Linguists, for all of them devised a different level of discussion beyond 'use of

*Revised version of the treatise published in: The Heritage, V-III, 2022.

language', the only concern of the linguists. There was, however, one school of Indian Philosophy, the Grammarian School initiated by Bhartrihari, which tried to interpret the world that is, thousands of years ago, in almost the same way as the linguists do it today. Taking by face-implications, they might look different on many counts. But a closer look might note surprising similarities between them.

INTRODUCTION

The present deliberation is not to advocate a particular philosophical system's indebtedness to another or any one of them as more acceptable; it is only to explore a few similarities between two schools of philosophy distanced by more than two thousand years.

The linguistic philosophy of the 20th Century, which was initiated by L. Wittgenstein in 1918 (first published in 1920, Eng. Tr. 1922), says that all questions regarding the possibility of external world or a so-called Reality that transcends appearance as to whether such a thing can be only ideal or can have extra-mental existence, etc, are meaningless simply because nothing beyond this world seems (to us) 'understandable'. Wittgenstein's Tractatus begins with this most obvious proposition from the linguistic point of view that 'the world is that is the case' (T.1). That means, before we start thinking about anything, we have our world around us as an undeniable fact. But this fact also entails this obvious fact that, all philosophic discussions, in the language of Gellner 'problems' (as in his 'Words and Things') about the world and for that matter about anything "are intimately connected with language and somehow emanate from it. They 'arisefrom' the use of words; and especially 'from the ordinary use of words…'

So, writes Gellner, 'the central ideas of Linguistic Philosophy' in a rough approximation is 'that language exists, plus some facts about language' and that is 'central for philosophy'.

Thus, we may say that, if the task of philosophy is to know about the world and other things that matter in this respect, we are to work only with propositions, for the simple reason that: To know about anything is to know whether a proposition about it is true or false. Later we shall see that we can know it only by referring, not to 'objects' or 'things' as is commonly believed but, to the simplest kind of propositions which are 'facts'. (According to Wittgenstein, 'the world is the totality of facts, not of things')

And about the 'simplest kind of propositions' he says, it is 'an elementary proposition' which 'asserts the existence of a state of affair' such that 'what is the case-fact-is the existence of states of affairs'.

We shall also see that this 'assertion' has no 'mirroring' or 'referring' function because these states of affairs are not material things, but things in 'a form of dependence', which again can be possible only in propositional forms.

It may be asked, can we talk of a world which is outside our mind and yet has no material properties? About this, again, let us refer to Wittgenstein who says that the world-substance is not made of material properties but of 'forms' presented by way of propositions. In his language: "The substance of the world can only determine a form, not any material properties. For it is only by means of propositions that material properties are represented..." (T.2.0231).

In T.011 he says: '.. it is essential to things that they should be possible constituents of states of affairs'. Now, let us take an example to demonstrate this T. Suppose, coming across a brown table in showroom, we say that 'this brown table is good', 'this table is one we were looking for', and so on. But before that, we believe that 'it is what it is by itself'.

But, if one asks why we so believe, we find that the belief is based on some simple assumptions that 'table is a thing that exists by itself', and, 'brown is a thing that exists by itself', and 'this table is brown....', and so on. And thus what we refer to is nothing but a totality of propositions, which are assumed true. But if asked, why do we so assume, we are obliged to mention few more facts in support, which are nothing but only more elementary propositions in claiming truth. The process can be further stressed, but nowhere without being in the form of some propositions, however subtle.

Now, if this Linguistic Philosophy can be seen as saying that 'propositions are only real', then this 20th Century philosophical trend has a striking parallel in a philosophical system of India dating back to 2nd Century BC. This particular philosophical trend is known as the Grammarian School of Philosophy and was initiated by Bhartrihari in a systematic way in his 'Vaakyapadiya' (hereafter referred as VP). To see this similarity we are only to look deep into the implications of the presentation of the system using some familiar terms of the age. These terms are more known for their metaphysical significance which traditionally includes, besides other things, the knowledge of the Ultimate Reality of the Universe beyond our day-to- day experiences. We shall see that this philosophical system took to a completely 'unusual' course of thinking about such experiences which resembles more the aforesaid linguists of the West than the traditional Indian thoughts, in liberating philosophy from the 'futile search 'for the 'transcendental'. The present deliberation shall proceed as follows:

Section I: The chief contentions of Linguistic Philosophy'.

Section II: The tenet of the Indian Grammarian School of Philosophy.

Section III: The basic points of similarity between the two systems distanced by more than two thousand years.

Section I: The Chief Contentions of Linguistic Philosophy

Linguistic philosophy, according to Gellner, 'is a certain cluster of views about the world, language and philosophy'. In spite of minor differences between these views, they have a considerably common view point which says: "The fact that language exists, plus some facts about language,... ". The unique approach of the Linguists towards philosophy can be had from a very interesting comment of Gellner, which says- "Linguistic Philosophy can conceive of its own activities as the euthanasia of philosophy. There is, in its view, no room on the map of knowledge for the kind of special insights that past philosophy claimed, or….strange questions with which it was preoccupied. "

Thus, it may be said that the Linguists' attempt to liberate philosophy from the futile battle of theories about the world, about the knower and the known, was on the ground that such theories miss the basic facts before anything, such as, 'The world is that is the case' and 'the world is the totality of facts, not of things' and so on. Indeed, the possibility of 'facts' replaces the possibility of things or of external objects, etc., which traditional philosophers vied for framing theories through ages.

Wittgenstein says: 'it is to things that they should be possible constituents of states of affairs'. What this implies is that, if states of affairs are 'objects in forms' and to be forms is only to be 'by means of propositions', then it follows that for all practical purpose there are only propositions and their use in language.

So, for the linguists, use of language is not only the most but the only important fact about man and his world. Outside language nothing can be meaningfully discussed, be it the question of the Absolute, of Physical entities, of morality, truth…in short anything that demands an enquiry. Clearly that marks a total departure from the path of traditional philosophy for which the most important deliberations are regarding those discarded objects of enquiry. According to the linguists, the aim of philosophy is neither the world, nor language, nor philosophy, nor mind as such. Its aim is to discuss all four aspects mutually entailing one another.

To explain the aforesaid position, let us take an example. M is a person who is so much a part of the world that is. For him the world is a totality of facts. And, we believe that there are stones, weights, gravitation, and numerous other things in the world. But, for M (as Wittgenstein sees it), the world(W) does not consist of 'stones' or 'weights' etc., but of facts where the said objects enter into relational forms as states of affairs, such as 'stone-is-rock-in-space', or 'stone-is-heavy' or 'stone-rolls-downwards', and so on.

That is, for M, the world (which is W+M), is equal to the sum total of facts (or states of affair) like 'SrK', 'SrH', 'SrD', ...(where S stands for 'stones', r stands for 'relation happening between', and H, D, etc. stand for 'heavy in weight', 'state of rolling down', and the like). In other words, W + M = SrR + XrY + PrQ + ArB +....n. Incidentally, these facts or states of affair like 'SrR' find place only if they are in the frame of language used by 'M'. (States of affairs can occur only as they are formed in some proposition, indeed elementary propositions, as Wittgenstein put it, occurring to man, and not in the world as such).

Now, about these forms in language, one might ask, had there been no physical objects in the shape of a stone, why the said forms were of that particular type and not of other types? Does it not imply from its being one form rather than any other in its place that, there was a material compulsion?About this, the Linguists would say, if one has to point to some of such extra- lingual stone-form, he has to say, 'Stone itself forced the said form', which is language again.

That the said stone is not a stone of the independent material world, it can be seen from this simple argument: The 'material stone', if any, would have made its presence to M as a whole phenomenon, i.e. as something with all it's so called material properties. But what matters for M about the stone at a particular moment is a particular fact or state of the affair (such as 'The stone is heavy') without taking into account another state of affair about it that 'Stone rolls down a slope' and so on.

Obviously not all properties are required to make the stone's presence to M. The stone is still very much a 'fact' of the world for M. It therefore follows that, for M the world does not consist of material stones, but, along with others, of the kind of states of affairs about it which are obtainable only in language (may be of very elementary form).

About this physicality of the world Russell, in his 'The Philosophy of Logical Atomism', says: "....take some science, say physics. You have there a given body of doctrine, a set of propositions expressed in symbols—I am including words among symbols... You do not know what is the actual meaning of the symbols that you are using ". [By the phrase 'actual meaning' I believe he referred to the 'whole of the physical object' meant by the symbol, as mentioned in the preceding paragraphs.

Again, in the next page, he talks about the physicality of objects as follows: "It is possible that there may be all these things that the Physicist talks about in actual reality, but it is impossible that we should ever have any reason what-so-ever for supposing that there are." According to him, there in the world are 'particulars and qualities and relations of various orders ...", and 'the only other sort of object you come across in the world is what we call facts, and facts are the sort of things that are asserted or denied by propositions'.

And talking about facts Russell almost follows Wittgenstein when he says: "... when I speak of a fact I do not mean a particular existing thing, such as Socrates or the rain or the sun." These particulars are 'facts which are the sort of things that you express by a sentence, and that these, just as much as particular chairs and tables, are part of the real world'. It may be mentioned that the said sentence (S) using an articulate form may not be sounded by M as is required in a communication; it may be un-uttered, un-sounded yet clearly occupying the in-mind form of its meaning-bearing grammatical syntax. It is equally important to note that the emergence of S in M in the world is a 'natural activity in the form of action-reaction' involving M in a particular situation. For example, in a classroom, 'chair-behind-table' or 'desks-in-front-of- table' are some facts that occur to M when he enters the classroom.

About how facts are related to a sentence i.e. language, Russell says facts make the propositions true or false. Thus it is not a 'table' or a 'chair' by itself that makes a proposition 'A man is sitting on the chair' and 'The table is swinging a man' true or false. It is, on the contrary, the facts about them, suchas 'C r M' (chair in a seating relation to man), or T r M (table in a swing relation to man) that make them true or false respectively.

Again, to quote Gellner: "… the world is just what it seems (and it seems so to an unimaginative man at about mid-morning), therefore, language is but a sect of activities in it." That is, man does not 'create' the world on the basis of ideas or thought (what an unimaginative man lacks). The world is what it is. But that does not make the world a host of inert objects either, for, that would deprive the world of its 'existence' to M that 'matters'. (The phrase 'unimaginative man' is used perhaps to guard the theory against being misunderstood for 'a kind of idealism').

Here the role of M is very important. He is not an instrument supporting the theory of 'esse est percipi'. What he does is just 'use of language' as a natural activity of 'simple response'. And this simple response is,for Austin, 'usage' in 'Other Minds', about which Gellner says: "This consists of saying that if there is conflict between a commonsensical way of speaking…and a theory, the latter must give way". This gives M a status different from both an inert piece of wood or the like and a constructing agent.

Let us, now state the tenets of Linguistic Philosophy as follows:

1. The world and its objects (things/substances) have no metaphysical worth in the sense of transcending the limits of propositional forms oflanguage. On the contrary, knowledge, according to Linguistic Philosophy, is, as Gellner puts it, 'after all something that occurs within the context of a language game', where 'language game' means the rules of use of language in a biological, psychological, social etc. context, and not any metaphysical context.
2. The old-fashioned metaphysical claims regarding 'objects of knowledge' is replaced by a natural route of understanding where the world is made only of facts, not things or independent objects. [According to Russell, 'facts belong to the objective world'].

3. Use of language by man is only real. 'There is.... no room on the map of knowledge for the kind of special insights that past philosophy claimed, or indeed for the kind of special, strange questions with which it was Pre-occupied'.
4. "All philosophy is a 'critique of language'..." in the sense that a proposition is the only 'model of reality as we imagine it'.
5. By analyzing a proposition we get the simplest ones, namely, the elementary propositions, "which consist of 'names' in immediate combination" and we do not know anything beyond this combination of names, because, as Wittgenstein says, "A proposition is a truth- function of elementary propositions", but "an elementary proposition isa truth-function of itself" (T.5). A similar view is expressed by Russell when he speaks of 'simples'. He says: "... I am speaking of something not experienced as such, but known only inferentially as the limit of analysis". And again, "... the old notion of substance ...can only be applied, if at all, to simples;...The essence of a substance, from the symbolic point of view, is that it can only be named – in old-fashioned language".].

Thus, for the linguists, language is the only thing that matters for man and his world. Without being in language nothing can exist. A mental state, say a state of anger for example, in a man's mind remains a 'non-entity' until it finds some articulated form/physical expression oriented either directly or in subtle form through the use of language.

Gellner Observes: "If words are tools used in the public world, then their meaning cannot naturally depend on something in a private or a transcendental realm." Here the two terms 'private' and 'transcendental' need special attention. Indeed, we can interpret the first as standing for 'a world that is of the ultimate possible state of the Idealist' and the second standing for 'a world that is of the Realist or even of the spiritual transcendentalist'.

Contrary to this, the Linguists take a naturalistic view of the use of language giving the world around man its required 'meaning', which simultaneously denies that language 'is a mirror of reality' and that from language 'one could infer the basic constituents of reality'. For them, says Gellner, 'Words mean what a given language, its rules, its customs say they mean, neither more nor less'. Thus the Linguists may be said to have maintained the old-fashioned metaphysics without the disadvantage of making transcendental claims within Linguistic Naturalism, which says, knowledge is a biological, psychological, social etc. process of the world.

With this brief exposition of the views of the 20th Century Philosophy behind, we shall now turn to the Indian Grammarian School only to see that many of the claims made by the former were also the central point of deliberation by the latter thousands of years ago.

Section II: The Tenets of the Indian Grammarian School

[**Acknowledgement:** This part of the exposition is mostly based on Gaurinath Shastri's 'The Philosophy of Word and Meaning' (Sanskrit College, Calcutta, 1959]. (*Note:* Duplication of a vowel is to indicate 'long' form of it).

The Indian Grammarian School of Philosophy in its formal construction began with Bhartrihari. Though the exact date of Bhartrihari is uncertain, Gaurinath, in his book, traces it with reference to Mahaabhaashya of Patanjali which is stated to be around middle of the 2nd Century B.C., and to Punyaraaja's Commentary on Bhartrihari's Vaakyapadiiya. According to Shastri, Punyaraaja not only mentions Samgraha, a collection of thousands of verses of which some were the fore-runner of Bhartrihari's views as a reference for Vaakyapadiiya, but 'actually quotes three verses from the lost treatise'.

The chief objective of the school was to show that the world is neither independent of, nor different from, words and sentences;

rather the latter make the ultimate reality of the universe meaningful to us. Let us refer to Bhartrihari's view of 'Eternal Verbum'(EV), Sabdatattva or Sabdabrahman, which is 'being' or existence in essence. This has a two-fold aspect, namely, the transcendent and the immanent. The transcendent one is something which, according to Punyaraaja, is Kaalashakti or Time-force that escapes all thought. So what is important for all practical purpose is its immanent character that matters, and it is the EV. The Eternal Verbum (EV) consists of the subject and predicate of all judgments. Bhartrihari says: "tasmaad arthavidhasas sarvaas shabdamaatraas sunishcitaah", which Shastri translates as, 'whatever passes current in our thought is determined by an articulate verbal form'.

These two aspects taken together implies, even if there is brute fact which 'is supposed to exist on its own' ('supposed' because it escapes all thought), such fact is as good as non-existent if it does not find an access to some articulate form of thought. Rather, says Punyaraaja, even a non-existent entity like 'hare's horn' has an objective occurrence if it finds place in the meaningful use of a sentence (sad api vyavahaarena…). [To be noted, a hare'shorn is a myth.]

Thus, what makes a hare's horn or a bull's horn existent is their use in meaningful sentence. He (Punyaraaja) says, the so-called objects of the world have no independent identity as x or y or any other thing. They are so differentiated from each other only because they are of different verbal forms. (… padaani prakalpya … vyavahaaram ihante). A simple example of how we confront only verbal forms and not 'objects' as such in our day-to-day activities can be had from a baby's reaction to, say, fire. The baby lacks the knowledge of fire of the form 'fire burns' (which is indeed the verbal form of the fact of fire's burning) and as he cannot distinguish it from the verbal form of a non-burning fact, may be a toy, he touches it with a smile (which should not have so happened had he known it as 'a thing fire, that burns'), and obviously cries by burning his hand.

Bhartrihari relates this verbal form of manifestation to any cognition whatsoever, be it of a supposed external object, or of a private feeling.

According to him, if a cognition (of something) is linked to an articulate form, it (what it is about) exists; and if it is not in articulate form, the said it is 'something' that does not exist. Even an elementary experience is not exempted from this rule 'anuviddham iva jnaanam sarvam sabdena bhaasate'. That means, even an elementary feeling of pain cannot be felt by a person unless he realizes it through a verbal form (for example, like 'I am in pain'), however un-uttered it might be. (A man engrossed in a dramatic climax of a drama going on the stage in front of him cannot attend to and feel the pinch of any defect of the seat, he was sitting on, without sacrificing his avid attention to some of the moments of the said drama. So, as long as he is so engrossed in what is going on there on the stage, the pinch is non-existent to him).

However, it may so happen that, in a particular case, the man immediately reacts to a pain suddenly caused by something, by sheer gesture without properly knowing what he was reacting to, that is, without having some language-form for the cause of his reaction. So one could argue that a verbal form is not essential for an object of knowledge. But, here Bhartrihari would reply, writes Shastri, even if such a piece of feeling (i.e. knowledge) were possible for argument's sake, it would be hardly distinguishable from a cognition or feeling that did not arise at all. [Bhartrihari says: 'Vaagrupataa ced utkraamed avabodhasya saasvati...etc.' (VP I.125). Here Bhartrihari maintains his difference from the Indian Idealists when he says: "Whatever progress we might have achieved in the different spheres of intellectual pursuits, is transmitted to us through words." Eng. Tr. of VP, I.1.26 by Shastri, The Philosophy of Word and Meaning, P. 6].

Thus, it may be said, if there were no language, i.e. no use of words and sentences as a form of communication between human beings, the world would have been reduced only to a host of insentient objects and, therefore, practically non-existent. Because, what is this world if it presents itself to another insentient object? Who talks about it? And, according to Bhartrihari, even if there were man, lack of the knowledge of language would reduce him to a wooden block 'kaasthakundyavat' (VP I.128).

Here the following question may arise: If a sentence (S) or the proposition it states does not refer to something outside it such that it could be adjudged T or F in accordance with its correspondence or lack of it, how the S can become meaningful? About this, Shastri gives Bhartrihari's view as follows: What is denoted or referred to by word is its own form coalescing with an objective fact such that there remains two apparently separate things coming together to form a larger group or system what we call the world.

Thus, according to him, in treatise on grammar a word sometimes denotes its own form and sometimes an objective fact. In his words, "... kvacid dravyam (rupam?) praadhaanyena avatisthate//loke 'rtharupataam shabdah pratipannah pravartate." (VP II. 131–32). [This may be translated as: a word is sometimes the fact of the world itself; sometimes, for the sake of man's understanding, is word of a sentence].

Thus, it may be said, Bhartrihari does not admit of any transcendental truth beyond our empirical and social communication. He says, transcendental truth is of little use for understanding empirical meaning of a word. "....na tena vyavahaara 'sti na tac chabdanibandhanam" (VP II. 141). That is, meaning of a word (and thus, of a S) depends largely on how one uses it under the paradigm of his subjective attitude and culture, because of which meaning of aword differs under different conditions or systems. If it were not to depend on how-where-and-by-whom used, the word would always mean the same thing as a transcendental entity should be. The word 'tiger' as a shout by a running man, and as uttered by a teacher in the class obviously have two different meanings. In the words of Bhartrihari: "yasya yathaiva svaadaraasana anusaarena pratibhaati tathaiva tasys sa shabdaartha iti.." (VP II. 144). In other words, 'meaning' of a word standing as a fact depends on its occurrence (in a particular situation).

Having said so, can we say that Bhartrihari and for that matter the Indian Grammarian denied any 'substance' that lay behind all verbal exercises? In this connection it would be worthwhile to mention his view of 'EV'. Regarding the apparent difference between form and matter, between word and import, Bhartrihari's explanation may be stated to show that after all he is a 'monist', though with a difference from the past and other contemporary philosophers. For him, both form and matter are but two forms evolving out of One Reality, namely the EV which, unlike the Brahman of the Vedanta, or the 'padaarthas' of the Realists, has its being only because it has its expression in language. He says: ekasyaivaatmano bhedau sabdaartha avaprithaksthitau (VP II. 31), which means, name and meaning of word and its import lose their different identity when considered for the real nature of both. An entity is its name: in spite of apparent difference, if no name to manifest, the entity does not exist at all. The difference between the vaacya and the vaacaka (the entity and its name) we experience is only empirical, not real. "nanu shabdaarthau Vaacya vaacakaaviti prasiddham…" (VP II. 32).

Now, it is generally believed by the Grammarians that words and sentences are the manifestations of the One EV. If so, then they are related as effects of the cause behind. About this relation between a cause and its effect, however, there is a debate among the Indian philosophers as to whether the two are identical or different. According to Punyaraaja, one school says that all effects are manifestations of their cause and, therefore, the two are non-distinct. Another school says, all changes in the language form are constructions of the intellect hence are different from the cause. And a third school opines that all these changes are the transformations of One Conscious Principle, implying thereby that they are apparent truth of One and non-dual Brahman (as the Vedanta says).

But if we look at what Bhartrihari said about the relation of these two, we find that he was not interested in the debate. He simply affirms that the EV is the material cause of the phenomenal world, meaning, on the one hand, the world is that is the case, and on the other, this world-process presents two lines of form and matter (which we already mentioned as word and import), implying their non-difference. Shastri interprets this position as follows: "In the opinion of Bhartrihari name and meaning lose their individualities on the transcendental plane, and it is only when the cosmic movements start that their difference becomes discernable". This opinion may be taken as stating that, their difference as cause and effect is only apparent. In reality they are identical. In the words of Bhartrihari: "kaaryakaaranabhaavena yogyabhaavena ca sthitaah" (VP I.24).

Now, does this concept of 'transcendental plane' take away the glamour of the Grammarian claiming difference from traditional philosophy? This needs a little more exposition of the concept of Eternal Verbum or EV. According to Bhartrihari, as Shastri presents it, the first manifestation of the EV, which he calls pashyanti, is madhyamaa, leading to subsequent verbal changes (i.e. words, sentences, etc.) called vaikhaarii. Interestingly, this pashyanti, believes Bhartrihari, can be attained, to use Shastri's language, 'only through determinate communion coming in the wake of the knowledge of chaste 'expressions' through a consummate and systematic study of grammar'.

> "tasya eva vaaco vyakaranena saadhutvajnaana-labhyena shavdapurvena..." (Punyaraaja commenting on Bhartrihari).

What Bhartrihari means by the above may be stated as follows: though of the form of something that is 'transcendent', EV or pashyanti doesnot really transcend all; on the contrary, it is how it finds its 'being' in 'correct'(chaste) use of language. Thus, says Shastri following Somaanandanaatha, Bhartrihari's "Supreme Principle, which is without a beginning and an end, which is consciousness in essence and indestructible and unchangeable, is verbal in nature and is called pashyanti."

Besides these features of the Grammarians, one more important concept used by them is of immense relevance so far our aim of the proposed comparative study is concerned. It is the concept of sphota which, according to Bhartrihari, is, firstly, an indivisible unit, and secondly, both an internal and external entity. It is eternal, purely spiritual or consciousness in essence but assumes externality through sounds, ".. yad antah shabdatattam tu naadairekam prakaashitam.. (VP II.30)]. Even our elementary feelings and sublime thoughts cannot be said to have occurred (to have of a deha or physicality) if they lack appropriate words. Bhartrihari says: "arthakriyaasu vaak sarvaa(n) samihayati dehinah "(VP I. 128).

Interpreting this view of sphota as purely spiritual or consciousness in essence, some recent authors have commented that Bhartrihari's theory of shabdaadvaita was 'based on Indian Idealism' (V.N. Jha: The Philosophy of Language in Classical Indian Tradition; Ed. K.S. Prasad, 2002) which, perhaps, is oversimplification. We have already seen that he always avoided the debate on idealism and realism. On the contrary, authors like Amitabha Dasgupta preferred comparing the concept of 'sphota' to the theory of 'sense' and its content as the meaning of a sentence, according to which, it is 'objective' in character because shared by many, but it is not situated in space – time as a physical object, nor is it fictitious, for, it can be grasped by competent speakers who use language ('Sabdabodha and the Epistemic Primacy of Sense). And this concept of 'sphota' as the content of knowledge is clearly distinguished from the Indian Idealistic concept of the Absolute, in which, according to K.C. Bhattacharya "we have only an indefinite relation between content and consciousness" ('The Concept of the Absolute and its Alternative Form'). He calls it 'Implicational Dualism' by which he means implicational relation between consciousness and its content., i.e. the Absolute, which has no definite term to qualify.

Now, if the two sections above are taken for the brief expositions of the views of the Linguists and of the Grammarians, we find that they come close to each other on many points. Let us see, in the following section, how that happens.

Section III: The Basic Points of Comparability between the Two

For the purpose of the aforesaid comparability, let us place the relevant points of the two systems together as follows:-

A. *The EV and the World of the Linguists*

Bhartrihari says, the Eternal Verbum or EV is subtle, meta-empirical, transcending all human experience, and pragmatic significance of day-to-day activities, even moral or religious values. It is non-relational, featureless, and changeless as transcendent. Its 'being' in essence transcends time.

But it is immanent in time in which it is subject and predicate of all judgments. And above all, 'whatever passes current in our thought' (which is equivalent to saying, whatever takes the form of thought), is determined by an articulate verbal form [sarvothah shabdena nirupyamaano vyavahaaram… (PR quoted by Shastri, p. 5).

Similarly, Gellner's comment on Linguistic Philosophers' view regarding metaphysics says, they maintain old-fashioned metaphysics within linguistic naturalism. [Wittgenstein: There must be objects, if the world is to have an unalterable form. (T. 2.026), and objects, the unalterable and the subsistent are one and the same. (T. 2.027)].

This stand of the Linguists suggest, the world is a safe, complete and stable world (not very different from the concept of a changeless cause of the world that is EV, the non-private and non-imaginary). [However, such contention evades the disadvantage of making transcendental claims.]

B. *Inter Social Communication and Language Game Model*

Notwithstanding the vision of the sages that is believed to transcend all, Bhartrihari is also of the opinion that our empirical and inter-social communication cannot be conducted with any transcendental truth. (… little use for understanding empirical meaning… Shastri, p. 10).

On the other hand, the Game-model of language says:

> ….ordinary concepts are adequate accounts of the world, for it is in terms of them that we have explained the use and place in the world of those various concepts in the Language Game… [This may be taken for what Bhartrihari meant by inter-social communication, for, according to the linguists, language is like a game which follows the rules accepted by all kinds of people including children or even stupid people.].

C. The concept of Sphota and of the Elementary Proposition

According to the Grammarians, a sentence is indivisible (for the opposite leads to infinite regress), and is called Sphota which is an internal entity, purely spiritual and assuming externality only when it is revealed by sounds. (VP.II.30). So a sentence as Sphota is the simplest form in which we come to the presence of EV (which is another name for the world for man) and is consciousness in essence.

Similarly, according to Wittgenstein, the simplest kind of proposition is the elementary proposition which makes a proposition T or F, but the elementary proposition is the truth- function of itself. This amounts to saying, the world that finds its meaningful existence in language is ultimately non-material and consciousness in essence.

Russell's view of logical atoms in forming our knowledge may also be mentioned here as supporting our view that we have stated about the Linguists so far. He says: '… you are not concerned simply with the question what is true of the world, but what we can know of the world '…..' Last residue in analysis are logical atoms and not physical atoms.'

D. *Language that is Verbal form is Only Real*

Regarding the nature of the Phenomenal World, the Grammarians and the Linguists have some basic difference which on last analysis shall appear only apparent. This may be seen in the following.

According to the Grammarians, phenomenal world has no independent existence, but is rather a reflection of the Absolute which is existence, consciousness and bliss, and upon which the phenomena is superimposed due to 'avidya' or a misleading creativity of thought. This contention reminds us of Monism of the Vedanta Philosophy.

According to the Linguists, the phenomenal world is the 'world that is', and hence, apparently in contrast to the Grammarian view, is the ultimate reality for man.

But it is interesting to note that, the Grammarians mark a dramatic departure from the traditional concept of the Vedanta regarding indeterminate Supreme Consciousness or Brahman when they say that Supreme Principle is verbal in nature and is called Pashyanti. Let us also add to this Utpaladeva's comment that 'the Grammarian has not conceived a stage higher than this'. (Shastri, p. 69)

On the other hand, the linguists make the world indirectly of the nature of consciousness when they say that world finds its existence only as 'facts', presenting themselves (the facts) in relational forms or states of affair which is basically possible only in verbal forms.

These are some of the aspects where the two schools come close to each other. There are other features too where the two are comparable. For example when both of them believe in contradictory situations. The concept of a new-born baby of the Grammarians 'who reaches out to a situation, notably without resorting to verbal forms' or the 'unimaginative man at about mid- morning', both pointing to non-verbal state of the world. But, as we have seen, Bhartrihairi is of the opinion that a brute fact is as good as non-existent if not in verbal expression [Tasmaad arthavidhaas sarvaas...etc. VP.I.120]. On the other hand, Wittgenstein admits of substance as 'what subsists independently of what is the case' and yet substance 'is not any material property (represented only by propositions)'. (T. 2.02311).

The list may be extended with more subtle or implied similarities.

If these comparable standpoints suggest that, like many other German scholars, Wittgenstein too had a chance to acquaint himself with the ancient Grammarian school of India, one might be interested to secure proof in favour of such possibility. But what is relevant here is that, the proximity of the two schools is a fact to reckon with. If the Linguists say that there is no room in the map of knowledge for any special kind of insight that past philosophy claimed, Bhartrihari too claimed that, transcendental truth is of little use for understanding empirical meaning of a word, read with this view of his that 'if no name to manifest, the entity does not exist', amounting to saying a 'Good Bye' to the traditional philosophy of his time. And, if these proximities occurred without acquaintance of the 20th Century school with the Pre-Christian school, then it is amazing.

'Argument' for a 'Higher Life' of the 'Common Man'*

INTRODUCTION

Before we engage in the dissertation, let me define the scope of the two phrases, namely, 'a common man' and 'a higher life'.

The term 'common man' I borrow from R.K. Laksman's concept of the same depicted in his iconic cartoon figure of the gentleman, who only gazes at the events, full of follies and the unjust happenings around him every day, feeling that they should not so happen. But he cannot help but be just an onlooker. (Courtesy: The Times of India). In other words, he is a man who lives a life of helplessness.

I, however, take this concept in a little broader sense to include also other classes of people where one toils as a loader in a market, works in a shipyard, where one is a poor slum dweller or a god-fearing rich man, a pauper, even to include one who indulges in crime to fulfill his desire, in short, every one of the society so far he is 'helpless' in the above sense.

While I say so, I, however, keep the mentally and physically challenged ones or one in a paralytic state out of this list for the simple reason that they cannot respond to any drive at their will.

So, going by the defined scope of a 'common man', we may divide them into three broad classes on the basis that, one belonging to each of the classes has the freedom to choose his way of living, but

* Revised version of the article published in Pratyaya, the Annual Journal of the Department of Philosophy, Tripura University, Agartala. 2008.

generally under limitations which he cannot overcome at will. The four classes(C's) may be as follows:

C1: The class to which the helpless gentleman of Mr. Laksman belongs. He has the ability to decide 'what should be the case to see the better of the present one'.

C2: The class of people whose activities are driven only by one drive, namely, the pleasure drive of any sort.

C3: The class of the poor people or the wretched ones who only struggle to survive.

C4: People who apparently are guided by outside force and not their own.

And, by the phrase 'a higher life', I mean 'a life' which is told to be not encumbered by our worldly needs, a life about which we learn from the spiritual leaders of the world, renouncing all drives towards worldly achievements, or have heard from the visionaries of the Idealist school of thinkers. It is a state of man's journey where, we are told, all dreams and desires culminate, where he attains a sort of 'light' from where everything else looks trifling. In simple terms, we may say, it leaves our 'present' behind.

Now, with these assumptions, we may proceed to ask, is there anyone of any of the classes above who turns a blind eye to the needs for constant improvement on the ongoing state of life he is living? Can he but work out a better condition for this life just because that is the best he can do as a common man? I believe there is none who does not want to change, because, man forms a part of Nature which is in constant change to adopt newer states forced upon by the inadequacies of the prevailing. [A relevant reference to this can be had from the author's "Truth a Work of Nature in Man "; Allied Publishers, New Delhi, 2006].

But the question is: is it possible for a helpless fellow of the society, or one who constantly works for immediate gains against this so-called growth process of man in the society, to strive for a better state where he can be relieved of the woes and burdens of the present? In the following dissertations we shall try to see how far it applies also to the transformation of the common man belonging to different classes to a higher state than the present.

Section I: Inadequacy of the view that the best way to happiness is to live with the present.

There are many who believe that the more one asks questions about the ultimate goal of life beyond his everyday experiences, the more one is lost in the blinding world of confusion. Their argument may be stated somewhat in this way: No one has given an answer to such queries that could be accepted as the last word in the process. Philosophers through ages have sometimes claimed to have found a final answer to such queries by way of 'sound' arguments. But their claims proved void for the simple reason that nothing can be known true under all conditions, particularly those that are yet to come, unless these are tautologies, if that is not supported by perceptual experience. Because, they argue, only direct experience can verify something as true for what is the case. And since we cannot 'see' the future, or anything that might happen but we do not know that it will, it is utter foolishness to attach any value to such 'knowledge'. On the other hand, they are always open to newer discoveries to replace the former ones by way of continuous process of observations and experiments, all pertaining to the presented situations.

Therefore, it is said, the best way to avoid discomfort in life is to refrain from asking questions about the unseen and to go on doing as the time and situation might immediately demand of an ordinary man. If, for example, my present state of affair demands that I do 'x' and avoid 'y' to produce happiness because that is the best that can be known for now, then that is the path to follow.

The above argument may suggest that it is just a common man's view and cannot be a part of serious philosophy. Even if it is so, firstly, there is no harm to be a common man, for ultimately all sciences and philosophy are meant to deliver truth for mankind, the majority of which are the so-called man of 'common sense'. And if an intellectual exercise is found to serve no purpose of man and woman in general in their day to day experiences, then such exercise is futile if not harmful. To use Hume's language: "...Commit it then to flames for it can contain nothing but sophistry and illusion". [An Enquiry Concerning Human Understanding: David Hume. Oxford 1902. P165].

However, the 'common man approach' got nod of another class of philosophers. According to them, 'the best way of living is to live with present'. The Caarvaaka school of ancient Indian Philosophy opined that, since all our knowledge are susceptive to doubts unless decisively verified by immediate perceptual knowledge where we see or touch or hear or taste or smell the object of knowledge directly, there is no point going for such knowledge. Abandoning the present for the sake of something that supersedes immediate perception is utter foolishness. No thought of the future, no morality that denies the immediate, no transcendental truth, if no one has ever experienced that. The message of this school popularly ran as follows: 'Enjoy life to the brim as long as you live without caring for what may happen in future'. In Sanskrit, the counterpart of it is: enjoy 'ghee', which is a costly butter-like delicacy, even by incurring 'rhina' or debts, and be happy so long as you live. This amounts to saying that man shall do best by 'living with the present'.

Greek philosophers (like Protagoras) held almost a similar line of thinking. They strongly upheld the view that 'man is the measure of all things'. His experiences, his emotions and sentiments, his value-judgments relating to his biological existence, his yearning for pleasure and abhorrence for pain, all these day-to-day features of life demand that he places his own feeling about something above everything else. In short, egoistic hedonism of any form rests solely on this argument that man's worldly existence is the prime concern for any theory about 'good or bad', about pleasure or pain. They would say, 'what is a good if one does not feel good about it?'

Many 19th and 20th Century philosophers too believe that all abstractions at the expense of man's 'present' is utter disregard for the 'Individual' that the man is. According to them, all abstractions including those that tell of the 'essence' of human existence are non-caring for the man concerned. It is non-caring because, they say, even mathematics is the creation of the human being and yet contains such abstractions that do not go with his experience. For example, that 2 +2 = 4 is supported by such practical experience where any two things added to another two practically make four things (of whatever kind) for him. But we shall see that such abstractions are non-caring for actual human experience if other conditions do not support it to happen. To use the words of Kierkegaard, from the fact that they always take off from the human reach because of which his existence becomes infinitely indifferent. Let us demonstrate a case. 2+2 as abstract numbers perfectly equal 4, but does not care whether practically 2 units of things added to two more will make 4 units there. In fact, it may not make four in some occasions. An earthen pot holding 2 liters of water will not hold 4 liter if 2 more liters are poured in it, if there is a hole at the, say, 2 liter level.

Kierkegaard thinks, abstract impersonal thinking may have some value in specific disciplines but is wholly inapplicable to the human situation. In his 'Journal' he writes: " Let it deal with plants and animals and stars but to deal with human spirit in that way is blasphemy, which only weakens ethical and religious passion." Schiller, the pragmatist, placed 'man' before everything else. In his 'Humanism' (1903) he constantly reiterates that truth and reality are man-made. He hailed Protagoras for his straight-forward view that 'man is the measure of all things'. In refutation of Bradley's famous thesis of ' appearance and reality', that opposes his pragmatic view, Schiller argued, even Bradley used pragmatic criteria when he had to decide between 'here and now' judgments or judgments at the level of appearance. In his 'Personal Idealism' (1902) he went further to deny that 'there is an objective world given independent of us and constraining us to recognize it'. And, however success the idealists might claim of themselves in proving the Absolute, ultimately even they are forced back on a merely human understanding to make it intelligible.

Let us, then, summarize the views stated in the above as follows:

> Man must be the measure of all things around his 'present', his perceptions here and now, his feelings of immediate pleasure and pain, attachment for pleasure and abhorrence for pain with lack of interest for what is believed to lie beyond. In short, he cannot ignore the man of today. The Absolute (or the Supreme Self, as some would prefer to call) with all its metaphysical bona fide to glorify human life is useless just because it lies beyond the grasp of our perceptual identity of today.

Section II: Why man's perception is not as perceptual.

The basic propositions of the theories discussed above may be formulated as follows: man must live with the present; whatever he sees or perceives around him here and now are all that matters; and hence the rest may be committed to flames if that contain nothing of his present. Let us see why these propositions upholding perceptual experience as the sole source of knowledge may be rejected.

Not going for the usual arguments of the rationalist, the idealist or the like against such naïve realistic views of knowledge being 'only perceptual', we shall turn to the basic inadequacy of such claims.

Knowledge cannot be limited to mere perception for the simple reason that it would make knowledge impossible. Because, firstly, perceptual knowledge of things comes from the operation of sense organs, and sense organs can hardly be trusted for the right view of a thing. What A sees of a thing (and believes that it is the right view), may not be the same for B or C seeing the same thing. A very handy example is the visual perception of the size of a hill by three persons standing at different distance-points from the hill. The hill presents three different views of its size to these three men. Even if they view it from the same point, their vision can hardly agree because of their possible difference of vision power. And if, say, they are called upon to view it through a binocular such that their vision is mechanically adjusted as having the same view of the object, their vision of the thing might still vary with the improvement in precision of the instrument. And there is no limit to such improvement.

Let us talk of mathematics. There are lots of 'objects' in its study which we ordinarily work on as perceived but which are actually not. For example, we 'see' a geometrical point on a sheet of paper. We give a name to identify it too. But a 'point' by definition is only an imaginary position not occupying any space or dimension in actual terms, therefore, no question of 'seeing' it.

Secondly, and that is more important, perception of an object needs a 'construction work' with the help of elements that are perceived along with some more elements that are not perceived at that moment. Philosophers have called this phenomenon of perceptual activity 'the inferential element in perception'. Blanshard in his 'The Nature of Thought' writes: "Let the reader try an experiment. Let him look to any object in the room and identify it as a book, table, chair, or flower-plot, and let him then introspect. Did he or does he, in perceiving the flower-pot, have in his mind images of its unseen side and its weight and …?"(Vol.I.P85). If, according to him, the answer is 'yes', then he is using those elements by some intellectual exercises to supplement the object of his perception. He writes "Perception involves not merely the presence of something, but also the taking of something as present which is not actually sensed…" (Ibid, p. 85). And Russell, writing about acquaintance and description of things, says: "There is no state of mind in which we are directly aware of the table; all our knowledge of the table is really knowledge of truths, and the actual thing which is the table is not, strictly speaking, known to us at all." (The Problems of Philosophy 1973, p. 26). In other words, when we believe that we 'see' a present object in its entirety, we actually do a construction work involving elements that are not present in front of the eyes.

One might argue against this contention that there have been attempts to break through this limitation, if at all we think so, where the 'not-present' is perceived simultaneously with the 'present' without any 'construction'. Picasso, for example, is one who uniquely drew paintings on the canvas which presented both the facing side of the object along with sides that are not facing. His 'Woman with guitar' or 'Man with a Violin' are two of the best examples of this attempt. Looking at these paintings we see the object in its entirety without toiling for any so-called construction.

But a little examination of the basis of this claim reveals that, firstly, Picasso did it only in a symbolic way leaving the grasp of the whole matter to the imagination of the viewer. He who lacks imagination, to him either the painting does not present the object, or if it does, it does so in a distorted way. To quote Blanshard again: "A painter might possibly recall one or two- but if so, his state would be more than merely perceptual". (Ibid, p. 85).

Secondly, in a state of perception what happens to a man is that he takes for granted that so and so is the case, that a material thing exists here and now, that it has a shape or look of such and such kind, and that it is 'x'(a name), all pertaining to some intellectual work. To use the words of F.H. Price: "what is taken for granted is a set of propositions "(Perception P.166). Not that one is always conscious of it, rather it can hardly happen consciously, for the whole work takes place automatically. Only thing is that this automotive act is processed by the faculty of his intellect in a subtle way. This is also one more reason why, when other conditions supposedly remaining the same, two man perceive a thing differently. A moving star in the night sky is viewed by a man of faith in the 'will of God' as a piece of Divine Wonder, whereas a man with scientific background views it as a change of orbit by the celestial body, both oriented by the process of thinking the two man they are accustomed with.

Section III: The Journey of a Common Man from Perceptual Encounter to listening to the Voice from within for something 'different'.

Let us, then, say that whether a philosopher or a painter, a scientist or a superstitious person, a saint or an evader of tax, a political messiah or the one exploited by him ... every man in his activities is guided by some intellectual exercises in their responding to the demands of the situations of the world he faces. He who believes that his perception of the present state is the only that matters for he has to ensure what is best for the particular situation he faces, he too takes to looking beyond what he is just faced with.

This he may do knowingly or unknowingly, but only such looking beyond ensures an effective confrontation. A Mumbaikar, whether in IIT Campus or in the slum area of Dharavi, faces water shortage during a particular period of the year. What he does is, he makes his present comfort (of getting uninterrupted water supply) more comfortable by making some provision for the same in future, without which he does not properly enjoy his present comfort. He stores water for the no-supply days of the week to come. This effort of his shows that, everyone believes that if he goes only by his present achievements of the moment, he cannot make even his present worth living. In fact, while living with the present, he needs to protect himself from all possible hazards including those that are not immediately present but are believed or thought of, and so 'known' to happen in future.

This indeed is a process of 'conclusion' arrived only by a decision-making process. And the more a man is mentally developed, the more he is inclined to a sound intellectual way of looking at things for the simple reason that his perceptual world makes way on all fronts to the rationally more 'useful' one. Again, since the process cannot stop there without contradicting the very purpose of the on-going process, he is led to a more comprehensive view of the whole endeavor. We shall see that it is this man within every man who supersedes primarily the belief in the infallibility of perception and then, in the same way, of intellect that think only of the near future. In other words, beginning with small start, he gradually embarks on an endless journey.

We may classify this journey as four **grades** of 'ascending' on the basis of what is the case when one confronts a situation. Let us mark them as follows:

G-I: Knowing what is apparently true and remains so for some time but very soon found not to work. G-II: Knowing what is practically true in the sense it successfully works in the world he faces today as well as in the days to come. G-III: Knowing what is rationally true in the sense that it is the inner truth of I and II that necessitates the growth process involved in them. The object of such knowledge, that is, the truth, may not normally be seen by an ordinary man. It only comes to him while pursuing I and II.

G-IV: Knowing the Supreme Truth which is nether G-I or G-II, and which also supersedes G-III to provide a more comprehensive view taking into account all the other three.

About these grades, we may say that, G-I stands for an unreflected and fragile sense perception, G-II stands for perceptions supported by some mental exercise of assessment, evaluation, etc. and G-III is based on elaborate rational exercises irrespective of their day to day applicability. But if we look deep into the meaning and significance of a state of knowledge, we find that even G-III is not sufficiently equipped to quell the growing discomfort of a man to remain limited by it. One who is in this process (of transformation), naturally develops a need for the acceptability of each of the state with reference to a lasting value.

It may be asked, how is it possible that something emerges from its preceding states where the seed of it cannot be said to be present at all! That this is not impossible, it can be seen in the following findings. Regarding reproductive system (in the bio world), sciences tell us that DNA is an acid in the chromosomes in the center of the cells of living species and that it determines the characteristics passed on from both parents, acting in combination, to their children. But from a Research Bulletin issued by the University of Iowa (May 3, 2007), we learn that, mutation occurred in sperm cells of a father, who does not have autism, passed the condition on two of his children. That means, this combination theory does not hold good in every case. So it is not a must that for something to emerge out of the preceding state, the seed of the same must be present in it. We may say, a phenomenon prevailing in Nature called 'man' may also strive to evolve out something (here it is aiming at something not ordinarily grasped by his present) which ensures an 'improvement' on the present 'frustrating' state.

Now, regarding the grades, while G-I and G-II are commonly attributed to the common man, G-III and G-IV are believed to be where the more gifted ones tread. (Incidentally, people belonging to the latter also cannot stop before reaching the highest that survives all skeptical doubts. It is an endless process, and is driven by every bit of success it meets in the way. Transition from G-III to G-IV, that is, from the scientific and logical world of the discrete to the all-comprehensive knowledge of the 'best' is subtle but irreversible for the simple reason that the matter comes from the eternal dissatisfaction associated with the former.)

But our present concern is about the common man whichever group he may belong to.

We have already seen that the growth process is a natural phenomenon. And so far man is concerned, it works in different ways for different sections of people. Let us see how this contention can hold true for the four classes of common man, we listed in the beginning.

Section IV: The process of Transformation in Common Man.

In this section, we are going to see if one belonging to this class can also have, in his living, the seed for a 'search' of the ' higher' in question that is supposed to be so different from his present one.

C1: A gentleman of this class is not blind to his inner voice telling him what is right or wrong, and is theoretically free to follow the message to secure a better of the present. But soon he finds his freedom is limited. But, nevertheless, we find that his endeavor goes on. We have seen how it drives a Mumbaikar to look beyond the present. He may also go beyond his day to day solutions by taking resort to intellectual exercises, observing religious rituals, or many of such other means which are not confined to practical achievements only. He is a compromising fellow even at the cost of conceding the wrong he knows in place of the right, for the sake of peace. He bears with the present, may sometimes also be with the thought of the future. As the Mumbaikar mentioned earlier.

And this is from where he begins to look further.

For this he might look for some isolated moments with a vast canvas of nature around him, or may be an adventure through the rugged terrains of a challenging mountain where he touches some kind of feeling of 'height' that he strives for. Sometimes he may even join crowds for the first time in life to protest a genocide in Tien-aan-men Square or for that matter anywhere in the world. These are apparently meaningless exercises so far his prime drive is concerned. But from these he gets something more than what he was busy with. And once the process starts, it is natural that he looks more and more for that 'different' life, because that is the basic drive in him, the drive to get more, now only with a change in the center of his interest. He represents that section of the people who in great numbers often crowd in a temple, a mosque, or a church, in art galleries, musical soirees, or a cricket match, and such other places where he gets the touch of something 'different'. Not that he has any clear idea of what he is going to finally achieve by these acts, but it takes him back to listen to the call of the person in him. He becomes more and more skeptical about infallibility of his perceptual world of here and now. He is inclined to truths of more lasting value.

It can be said that the drive is always there, only subdued by the immediate demands of everyday life. Radhakrishnan says, it is the spirit that drives him. He writes: "The spirit looks on disinterestedly, its delight is pure and free;...when the supreme light in us inspires the intellect, we have genius, when it stirs the will, we have heroism; when it flows through the heart we have love, and when it transforms our being, the son of man becomes the son of God "(An Idealist View of Life, 1979, P. 162).

C2: One belonging to this group is he who is driven only pleasure drive. One of the strongest of such drive, according to the Psychologists, is the sex drive.

It is so strong that, instead of superseding the immediate, it sometimes indulges even in criminal acts to realize it.

Obviously, such a drive cannot be taken for one that prompts transformation of the kind we are talking about. But Psychologists have found that, even in such cases the incumbent gradually realizes that either his lust goes on increasing without delivering the desired all-fulfilling sense of achievement (no question of complete freedom from the 'cry for more'), or it starts tormenting him by way of a total boredom. He then, says the psychologist, goes for sublimation of the said drive. Freud is of the view that, the person's concern shifts from primary drive for gratification to applying secondary process, thinking to gratify desire symbolically and intellectually by means of friendship, love... [Prof. S. Freud: A General Introduction to Psychoanalysis. Eng. Tr. G.S. Hall. N.Y.]

The pleasure drive of any sort can take a person believing only in it to no better a place then this realization that the goal of 'the more the merrier' finally falsifies itself by the frustrating realization that there can be no end to such 'more'.

C3: Coming to the state of this class, we may say that this, perhaps, is the largest of all. It is the class of people who are poor and deprived of all sorts of comfort of life, of adequate food and money, of normal respite and enjoyment, of clothes in winter, a roof in the rains... in short, those who live a subhuman life. It is the class about which, it is said, one belonging to this class has nothing to lose. So there cannot be any question of any sense of insecurity searching for its relief.

He lives in a slum, a roadside shanty, or under the busy flyover of a sprawling habitat. He toils the whole day just to live, such that there is literally 'no time to stand and stare' for something other than completing his present task.

The question that may be asked here, can we say that this section of the common man too can afford to have the same drive for something which we may call 'higher'?

Apparently the doubt expressed in it is quite pertinent. In fact, it might look like a luxury for one belonging to this class. But on a closer view, we shall see that, he too is a believer in a kind of something which supersedes his present. That may not be called an act of listening to the voice within. In all probabilities, it is a different kind of 'fulfilment'. It may be the case that he starts believing that all his sufferings are his destiny. But nevertheless, that takes him above his present. At the end of the day, he looks for a few cosy moments when he can breathe with a relaxed mind and body, ha can sing a song of a hit Hindi movie, make love, share happy moments with a dear one. The difference of his attitude is evident. While he lived the whole day for survival only, this is the time which he longs for itself.

May be, he does nothing of the above but only savours a full bottle of country liquor. But maybe he does so only to leave behind all woes of the day's struggle. And if that is the case, then would it be unfair to say that he strives to go over the whole day only because he has something for him at the end ' very different in kind', where there is not a shade of his day's life !

C4: However, a few apparently belonging to this class, namely Class 3 above, are people who are found to be driven by such forces which overpower their normal thinking. For example, when one of this class starts thinking of the world beyond the rows of the hutments he is forced into, his peace begins to shatter. He becomes angry. He wants an end to this sorry state his by any means. The fallout of this is the worldwide unrest which is exploited by the religious fundamentalists and the dishonest politicians to fulfill their own 'missions'. This is one enemy of peace which gradually overpowers the man's own self. He falls prey to the external drive which only decides his way of life.

It may be mentioned that this man is somehow dragged away from the aforesaid process of natural transformation in him. He, on the contrary, starts believing that he has nothing to lose, the least the call of the spirit in him. He even starts believing that annihilation of his own existence is a matter of pride if it can destroy peace around.

Hence this section of the common man may be said to defy the so-called process of growth in him, for he has no liberty to listen to his own voice of any sort.

But a closer look will reveal that even he takes to the course of being dictated simply because he feels that only this will lead him to some achievement which is the highest one can achieve. He too is indeed in search of the 'better' we are talking about.

Section V: Scope of Argumentative exposition of the assumption that a Common Man too strives for transformation of his self.

The Gita says we are not to lose hope in any way, for, man is ultimately the master if his own fate through all his thoughts and activities. It is he who chooses the right or the wrong path to achieving a goal, and no goal can be final unless it delivers the coveted state of unthreatened fullness. Therefore, even if his present does not 'permit' him to think for such an 'unseen' state of life, nature will take its own course, may be taking a longer time. What happens in him is stated by the Gita as follows: "Senses prevail over bodily action-reaction. Mind supersedes senses, intelligence supersedes mind. But what works above intelligence is the soul" [Sect.3, Verse 42; Eng. Tr. S. Radhakrishnan.]. Radhakrishnan writes: "In the depths of the human soul lies something which we rationalize as the search for truth, a demand for justice, a passion for righteousness. This striving for truth and justice is an essential part of our life."[An Idealist View of Life (1979), p. 38].

It is true that nothing can be finally good either for the individual or for the society as a whole if the living conditions do not change. No blind faith, no blind allegiance; one is just to listen to the call of his conscience fighting out the right against the wrong in his day to day activities. But, if the principle of constant change in Nature is at work, then it cannot stop at one point. May be the approach of individuals belonging to different classes differ, but, it is an ongoing process. A saint or a sinner, a prince or a pauper, an executive in an office or an excavator in a mine, all are on a path to that same goal.

And that the deprived ones shall finally join the process is not just an elitist imagination; nor this transformation a luxury for the poor and the unprivileged. On the contrary, every man is common man in the sense he is a part of Nature's continuous process of evolving out more and more congenial states in its different fields (the equivalent of which in 'human field' is a 'a higher state of life'). He has to respond to the demand of Nature itself and cannot but follow this course of the process. Only some might begin to work for the transformation consciously, others might even not 'know' that they are already in the process. But if at any point of it one feels the inevitable difference that is supposed to show up in his otherwise mechanical and/or un- reflected functioning, he is very well in the main stream of the thriving human race.

One might say, these observations only initiate, if at all, an enquiry, but cannot be taken for argument in favour of the concept of 'higher life' in a common man as such. May be so, but I think, we should not have any problem with that. Because, are not many of our theories built on observations only? If that is true, let these observations initiate the argumentative steps towards finding the truth of the poetic belief '.... they also serve who only stand and stare'. May be we have to wait for that day to come. But, nevertheless, it is better to wait than to submit to despair.

The Karma Principle of the Gita and the Nature of Human Action[1]

ABSTRACT: Besides its chief message of the salvation of human beings, the Gita also highlights the role of a common man to the effect that he by nature searches for a better and yet better form of life such that it overcomes the limitations of his immediate present.

INTRODUCTION

In the Mahaabhaarata, Arjuna in the battlefield of Kuruskhetra refused to raise his bow (gandiva) against his revered kin standing as opponents on the plea that, even so achieving unchallenged supremacy on the earth it was not to deliver freedom from all earthly pangs.[2] Then Lord Krishna, his mentor, convinced him to go ahead by uttering the truths related to man's life and his action. This ran through 18 sections thus constituting the text of the Gita. Here, however, we shall primarily discuss only those verses of karmayoga, with occasional reference to a few others, which may be relevant for the common man of today so far their life and actions are concerned.

These verses are: (a) that no one can refrain from action even for amoment; (III/5). (b) that even the sustaining of the biological existence (the sariira) of a person cannot afford inaction for a moment (III/8); and (c) that only by maintaining the required active role one attains siddhi or the ideal state of life. (III/20).

---

[1] Revised version of the paper of same title published in The Heritage; Issue No. 2, Vol. I, 2011.

[2] The Gita II/4-8. Note: All references of the Gita shall be followed by its section and verse number.

In the coming sections of this deliberation we are going to examine two probable hypotheses based on the above. These are: 1. The principle of action of constantly evolving better and better conditions for him as the Gita envisages is a natural drive in the sense that man does not 'adopt' it by way of a 'special' afterthought, but that he is naturally endowed with it right from his birth: and 2. It happens to all men irrespective of how he is placed in the society.

I

Man Constantly Works for Betterment of his State

To begin with, let us consider the implications of the verses mentioned above telling that man cannot but be in a process of action and such action is naturally and compulsorily directed towards achieving an ideal state of life. The questions that need to be answered are: firstly, is non-stop action a reality and necessity of life? And, secondly, can such action be said to be for the 'betterment' in the sense in which the Gita speaks about it? In our day to day experiences we find that there are people who work for some return but do not enjoy the real fruits thereby produced so that it could deliver a 'better state of life' for them. On the other hand, there are people who do not work for themselves but improve their state of living by enjoying the fruits of the toil of the former. None of these two can be said to go with the spirit of the principle of action of the Gita; for, in the case of the former there is action but no real achieving of the fruit of the action, and in the latter, there is accomplishment of some goal but no action behind to accomplish it.

Again, let us consider a few more cases where the individuals concerned work for their betterment but cannot be said to work in the spirit ofthe Gita. A millionaire, for example, is always found to act in the way in which he can secure a berth in the fold of the billionaire. A starving person acts just for having one piece of bread a day. Again, a God-fearing man's action may be directed to achieving some sort of heavenly charisma that would make life a casket of fulfillment, whereas for the poet, the aim is to attain jasha or glory inthe world of literary appreciation, the 'garland' in Tagore's poem 'puroskaar'. In other words, every human being acts with some goal from his point of view. But such acts are not particularly directed towards achieving any kind of siddhi or the ideal state of life.

So, before we go for examining how human action is aimed at achieving an ideal state, we shall firstly see whether the proposition that manhas to constantly act as a 'demand of nature' is valid. For this, we may have alook at the biological world where the process of constant change in the formof development, however subtle, means 'life' for a living creature no matter whether a microbe or a plant.

A seed, for example, lives so long it maintains its germinating (i.e. growth) process through the principles of synthesis, assimilation, egestion, etc. [The principle of ankura kurvat roopatva of Indian Philosophy was based on this principle of a seed]. As soon as the seed stops the process, it is no longer aseed but something belonging to non-living class like a piece of earth. A human being is no exception, the only difference being, he can design his development process by applying reason and thought over the biological part working for him which the former lacks. But what is significant here is that he cannot but maintain this process of change to keep his life going. St. Thomas inhis Treatise on Man of the Summa Theological says that the human person tends innately to grow on every level, physical, psychological, social...; indeed he refused to accept that human person could be static. (Desmet, 1976)

We are thus led to seek answer to two important questions that arise here, namely, (1). Does a man by nature really work to improve upon his existing state out side the naturally designed course of action controlling everything on earth including all living creatures? (2). Does the phenomenon of constant change mean a growth process to the effect of achieving a better state of life?

Let us begin with the hypothesis of 'working for a better life'. If we turn to the overwhelmingly larger section of the people of the world, we find that they can hardly be more concerned with any imaginary future than their immediate present. A hungry man, for example, cannot think of anything beyond a piece of bread just as a drowning man cannot think of anything, not even the face of God he worships, beyond his immediate of ' a little air to breathe'. Thus the demand of addressing the immediate needs for a man is so natural so far his survival is concerned that there can hardly be any other 'demand of nature'. So, how it is that under all circumstances is driven to pursue the so-called search for a better life ignoring the present? That will be our prime concern in the next.

If we look at the basic nature of the said 'driving force' behind allhuman actions, we shall see that whatever be the state of his life, he acts onlybecause his 'survival' needs them to go on in order to create the right condition for it. Bergson, observes Russell, was of the opinion that ' life is one great force, one vast vital impulse, given once for all from the beginning of the world, meeting the resistance of matter, learning gradually to use matter by means of organization… seeking always the greater liberty of movement amid the opposing walls of matter.' (B. Russell on H. Bergson's Creative Evolution; The History of Western Philosophy). In other words, man's inherent life force alwaysdrives him towards something new and it is quite natural that this 'new' is more than what he already has. The Gita in Sect. II (31/33) says: If one does not adhere to his natural endeavor for the best ('the opening of the doors of Heaven') he falls from his nature (dharma). Here the Heaven symbolizes a higher state of life that satisfies all needs. That means man's endeavor for the said elevation is a natural phenomenon.

Now, what follows from these propositions is that, as everyone is in the process, it cannot for the sake of the same process stop short of producing a realization of some betterment beyond amassing some fortune of utterly temporary nature. Because, any happiness of perishable nature generates greater sorrow by way of fear of losing it any moment. Thus further advancement in the process takes one to the yearning for a state of fear-free happiness that is of permanent nature. What constitutes the latter, we shall discuss in the coming sections. But presently we can say that, once he knows the difference between the two, he naturally goes for the permanent one as his final goal. In the beginning everyone may not be very sure about the nature of his goal. But what is important to note here is that, man's striving for the 'better' is only a natural phenomenon. In the next we shall see how far human psychology is conducive in such betterment process.

II

How Far Human Nature is Conducive to Such Work

On the question of improvement, we have to consider two things. Firstly, when can a person be ready to for the so-called 'perfect state of life' in place of the ordinarily realizable immediate gains? And, secondly, can we say from our worldly experiences that a man shall be interested to take him to such 'perfect state'? I believe, before we answer the questions, we need to analyze the human mind and see under what conditions it is conducive to the required growth process.

It has been observed by psychologists, particularly the psycho-analysts that so far actions are concerned man differs from other animals for the simple reason that human actions are driven by rationally working motives as against the blind mechanical ones regulating the actions of the latter.

Basically, they observe, all actions are led by a 'pleasure principle' which aims at satisfying basic biological needs like food, sex, rearing the offspring, etc. But along with these immediate aims for pleasure, the motive behind human actions also aims at avoidance of pain, averting possible threat to security, etc. And it is this aspect of the drive that works in human actions even to sublimate and undermine his immediate pleasure. Freud writes: "… the mental process is automatically led by the 'pleasure principle…". But "Under the influence of the instinct of the ego for self-preservation, it is replaced by the 'reality principle' which without giving up the intention of ultimately attaining pleasure yet demands and enforces the postponement of satisfaction…". (S. Freud: Beyond the Pleasure Principle). We find that these observations of the psycho-analysts agree with the concept of karma or action of human being envisaged by the Gita in the verses we mentioned above.

Psychologists further say, contrary to normal belief, that a man's usual lusts and longings do really work out this kind of 'beyond the immediate' in his day to day activities, however subtle such working may be.

For example, Lindeswith and Strauss have shown that human motive is not limited to addressing the immediate only. According to them: "'Motive' has forward reference in time. It is concerned with purpose and with the anticipated consequences of acts." (Lindeswith & Strauss: Social Psychology). Looking from this psychological point of view, the proposition that 'man by nature cannot but constantly act towards improving his state' does no longer remain improbable. Rather this becomes his identity as a being who lives, no matter under what condition he does so.

Against this contention it may be said that in more slokas than not the Gita clearly states that this process of attaining a higher state of life (the ultimate of which is siddhi) can be achieved only by very special kind of act andby the people of such caste who are socially so stationed as to make them capable and eligible to perform those special deeds. Therefore, in the life of those who do not belong to those classes, this principle of working for the better cannot occur as a motive. But if we take a comprehensive view of all the sections of it, we shall find that it speaks more of confidence than frustration for any person on earth irrespective of his social status.

For example, verses 35 of section III says: "sreyaan svadharmah vigunah… etc." which Radhakrishnan translates as – Better is one's own law (of action)though imperfectly carried out than the law of another person carried out perfectly…etc., and interprets as " We have not all the same gifts, but what is vital is not whether we are endowed with ...but how faithfully we have employed the trust committed to us..." (S. Radhakrishnan: The Bhagavadgita). [In verse 34 it is elaborated that, whatever action is guided by the sense organs, is liable to attachment or abhorrence. The best way is not to be subordinated (basham) to them]. Verse33 emphasizes this truth of human action that even the wisest of them is bound by nature to act. Then follows the most important statement in this respect: prakṟtim yaanti bhutaani. (The entire universe is moved by nature)].

What these all mean is that man's constant endeavor to rise above his worldly limitations is in his nature itself and he need not fear that his acts may not be the same as is pursued by the gifted few. Incidentally, the message of Sri Aurobindo (Sri Aurobindo Birth Centenary Library, Vol.18) comes very close to this when he says that the embodied state through which the individual holds his creative role does whatever he can do to bring about the next step of evolution no matter what material role he plays in the society. In section IV (10-12), the Gita says: Man by whatever way he follows the path of karma or action to 'reach unto me' finally accomplishes his goal of siddhi. (Here 'reaching' the elevation of the Lord stands for a state of supreme completeness). And the success of human folk trying to achieve this siddhi through his actions is faster than by any other means.

Now, about how and for whom this 'process of improvement' is possible, the Gita says: he who is unperturbed in sorrow and unmoved by pleasure, who has left behind the impulses of anger, fear and attachment is the free soul who achieves eternal calm and peace in life (II/56-58). That means, total renunciation of worldly impulses like that of 'eat, drink, and merry', of lust andgreed, of a thought of revenge in anger or of losing nerves in fear. This is the only means to the condition 'ideal' for the said transformation. But can we say human motive shall pursue such an unbelievable path practically against his present to achieve something in future so unknown to worldly list of wants?

III

The Battle of the Present with the Future in different sections of the population which appears not to work for siddhi as the goal.

An exposition of the issue in question may begin with a piece of the author's experience in this regard. In the North-east Indian city of Agartala(like many other in the region) every year with the advent of winter several 24-hour long community kirtan (a form of singing the glory of the Lord Krishna) continuously for weeks together are held in the different market places of the city. Three groups of people are involved in the whole affair. The motive behind each of them is to secure something for their 'future life'. The groups are: (1) the singers who continue to sing in a relay method by batches at the top of their voice; (2) the business community of the market which spends lots of money to organize that; and (3) the devotees who gather around singing arena, normally in the evening and through the whole wintry night under the poorly covered area. Incidentally, the majority of the third group are widows and house wives of rather poor families who constantly encounter the pressing demands of the present with very little resources.

Now, judged by the required kind of action laid down by the Gitafor the purpose of securing an ideal state of life, we find that all of them aredoing some sort of renunciation in their respective role in the affair. For example, individuals of the first group sacrifice their physical comfort going through enormous strain; those of the second group their worldly pleasure equivalent to the portion of the wealth thus sacrificed; and of the third, sacrificing their hours of relaxation after day's works at home. But when askedabout what they particularly wanted to achieve by such acts, their reply differed from each other and curiously enough none of them said anything that matched working the siddhi program of the Gita. They replied as follows:the singers – earn financial security for that period of the year; the businessmen- to attract blessings of the Lord to ensure more smooth earning (maximum tax relief notwithstanding); and the devotees – peace of mind amidst all odds of daily encounters. Obviously there is no thought of a better state of life to the extent of siddhi of any sort in these actions.

The above may be an isolated observation, but if we look at human actions in general, we find that, however such activities are aimed at some kind of improvement over the existing state, such improvement does not mean achieving a state of life which might be called ' the ideal transformation of life'.

Let us consider cases where people may be said to indulge in the straightway act of 'renunciation'. They are found to do it with a view to have a secured future in this life or even in the life hereafter by way of sacrifices in thename of the gods, deities, the spirits, and so on. Some of the common items of sacrifice: shedding hair for life, giving up a most favorite food item forever, missing meals for hours every day for a certain period, and so on. Some may say that such activities are of the kind endorsed by the Gita itself as is stated insome verses of it. Foe example, the last part of verse 12 (III) says: taih dattanapradaaibhyah yo bhungkte stena eva sah, which means, he who enjoys the gifts given by the gods without returning them back is nothing but a thief. But it can be easily seen as activities practically aimed at averting the wrath of the gods for thieving and nothing to do with the stated movement towards betterment of the self as the Gita has set as the goal. In the same section (13 and 16) the Gita ranks these as lower kind of act compared to those that accomplishes paramagati or the ultimate elevation where one rises above his worldly inclinations towards securing wellbeing in his present state. The verses 19 and 20 say: one who works with no attachment to achieving any fruit of such action achieves paramagati, and that it was by sheer works (without attachment) that Janaka and others attained perfection. [asakto hi aacharankarma paramaapnoti purusah … karmenaiva hi samsiddhim aasthitaah janakaadayaha] (III).

Thus, what all these cases suggest is that, a normal man, if he at allworks for the betterment of his state, do so either strictly to improve his present or to thwart insecurity psychosis overcasting his present due to the fear of the sufferings in future. Evidently, such activities are not the kind that can really be called the one directed towards 'betterment process' of man's life. So the karma principle is generally not acceptable.

Then, does the Gita restrict the possibility of transformation process of human beings only to a kurbannaapnoti... etc., which means, he who performs only his 'duty' demanded of him by a station he is placed in of whatever kind, serves he path of virtue.

It is this message that the Puducherry Ashram of Sri Aurobindo has been putting in practice for the last hundred years.

IV

The Seed of 'Elevation' in Every Human Action

We shall now see, firstly, that even the activities mentioned in the preceding section have the seed of the same principle of 'growth' or 'elevation' towards an ideal state however different it may look from outside and, secondly, that people even without being specifically gifted or advantageously placed to act in their day-to-day life to serve the aforesaid karma sanskṟti or the principle of work.

J. Nehru in his The Discovery of India refers to this work culture ofthe Indian people by quoting Havell, who said 'In India religion is hardly a dogma, but a working hypothesis of human conduct, adapted to different stages of spiritual development and different conditions of life... a working hypothesis of human conduct must work and conform to life, or it obstructs life...' (J. Nehru: The Discovery of India). In the same book Nehru also wrote ' Behind it (the old Indian Social Culture) lay the philosophical ideal of India culture – the integration of man andstress of goodness, beauty and truth rather than 'acquisitiveness'. In other words, the truth of continuous striving for raising the state of living higher and higher is a practicality for Indian way of living. They do work with the spirit of the karma principle though may be without knowing that they are doing so.

Tagore referred to one of his experiences which he gathered while driving through some rugged villages of Bengal. His car needed water every now and then for the troubled engine and the villagers provided it from their paltry stock of drinking water that too refusing to accept anything in exchange when the reality was that those villages were passing through drought conditions. (R.N. Tagore: The Religion of Man).Tagore has cited this as an example of ' Man's Nature'. On many occasions a person, however disadvantageously stationed, rises to the state of performing an act which quite perceptibly follows the basic principle of the Gita of no immediate profit. But, even in cases where it exhibits the motive to the contrary, a closer look in it might reveal that it was observing the same spirit, though might be in a very 'different' way.

In fact, in the Indian subcontinent it does not require much effort to trace such instances where the common man whether privileged or unprivileged exhibits this kind of silently following the principle of karma in their everyday life in its real spirit. It can be noticed in other regions too. Here we would refer to another experience of Tagore when he was visiting Japan. In the midst of enormous material growth, the people of Japan was never divorced from the inner search for an everlasting ideal of life. He writes: ... in her art of living, her pictures, her code of conduct, the various forms of beauty which her religious and social ideals assume Japan expresses her own personality, her dharma, which, in order to be of any worth, must be unique and at the same time represent Man of the Everlasting Life.

And even the materialistic west does not lag behind realizing the inner truth of life. Talking about the apparently all-fulfilled life of the business community of his time, Nietzsche observed .... these business men too are slaves, puppets of routine, victim of busy-ness;

they have no time for new ideas; ... hence their restless and perpetual search for 'happiness' ... their vulgar luxury without taste... their sensual amusement that dull rather refresh or stimulate the mind· This frustrating realization, we may say, works as a natural reason to find the right drive for actually what they should try to achieve instead.

Thus we may say that, generally speaking, the majority of human beings while working to improve their life, in fact, act for a 'betterment' which supersedes their immediate worldly goals where such thought of 'betterment' works as a seed to reach siddhi envisaged by the Gita. Incidentally, about possibility of siddhi of karmayoga in ordinary life Swami Vivekananda said that the ideal of niskaama karma (action without desire for fruit) is difficult, for, normally every action of ours initially has a selfish end to meet. But if we start thinking about the worth of the goal with calm and perseverance, the extent ofselfish motives gradually decreases, finally producing a total dispassionate state of action. (Vivekananda Rachanaa Samgrha, Eng. Tr. by the Author).

Now, before we draw a conclusion about the three hypotheses set at the beginning, let us mention three exceptional cases where the motive behind the act is avowedly to the contrary of the principle of 'elevation'. These cases are: (1) Of the terrorists who indulge in mindless killing and destruction running after some sort of ill-conceived 'dream'. (2) Of the dictators and political/capitalist oppressors who are found to indulge in any kind of anti- human act to acquire more power, wealth or supremacy over others; and (3) Of the die-hard criminals e.g. the rapists, contract killers, etc. (The list is not exhaustive in any way).

Without elaborating the contrary nature involved in the activities ofsuch people and the like, it can be clearly seen that these do not conform to the aforesaid basic principle of human action. How, then, are we to support our thesis that there is a 'seed' of 'elevation' in every human action?

V

Validation of Our Hypothesis and Concluding Remarks

We have so far tried to see that two hypotheses, namely, that man is bestowed with a drive for betterment of his state right from his birth and thatthis drive works in everyman irrespective of how he is placed in the society.

This drive works in most cases of human action. We shall now see how it worksin all cases including apparently exceptional cases as the three mentioned in the preceding section.

The 'dream' working as a drive behind the first group of people may be viewed from an average standpoint as highly misconceived and detrimental to all human values. But their striving for realization of the dream renouncing all normal human demands of the present (like a family, personal security, comfort, etc.) speaks of the fact that man's basic principle of karma works heretoo in the form of renunciation of some sort on the one hand and setting a goal beyond the present on the other, in spite of the fact that the goal so set does not rightly help him. But one thing may be inferred here that would again support our view. In such cases a correction of the goal may not be ruled out through a realization of its futility.

And if that takes place, which has been observed in many occasions, it can so happen only if the principle of inherent urge for betterment of state is true.

About the second case, a possible defense of our hypotheses maybe as follows: History tells us that dictators and other political/ capitalist oppressors have in many instances come to 'share' their power / wealth with the 'people' for sheer survival through changing conditions of the scenario. The white rulers of erstwhile Pretoria regime, the colonial rulers of the British Empire, scores of dictators of Europe and Asia are some such examples of transformation. One best example is Ashoka, the great emperor, who renounced everything when he was on the grabbing spree of kingdom after kingdom. And, about the capitalist's society, for example, Russell, in Unpopular Essays, wrote: The relation of buyer and seller is one of two parties who are both free; it is most profitable when the buyer or seller is able to understand the point of view of the other party. This obviously is an attempt to ensure the best by 'sharing', a very initial form of 'renunciation'.

It is true that this principle of karma aimed at the best is not yet found to be universally working. (We do not know if the mind of the 'Great Dictator' Hitler changed in his last days in the bunker because of the horror of being left with only him to curse). But the transformation in some cases suggests that it is the most undeniable of principles for man to pursue in order to exist and to flourish. The emergence of the United Nations is one way of proof of this change towards sublimation of the attitude working against it.

Similarly, about the third, who knows a Valmiki, the great poet of Ramayana is not the destiny of every dreaded dacoit Ratnakara?

Thus, in respect of our hypothesis (1) that the principle of karma constantly evolving better and better conditions for man's life is a natural drive from birth, and (2) that it happens to all men, the following observations may be made.

Firstly, they are not improbable. Even before one knows the truth of the message of the Gita, or for that matter, any other great educator of the world, one cannot but contribute to the process of continuous elevation of himself for his own survival in a better world, for, that is the natural law of all creature. Only their stages may be different.

Secondly, even where cases fall outside the former, those may be considered as cases of 'natural calamity' as some of them occur in a temporarydefiance of nature's law. Nature always restores its own law after each calamity. Similarly, for the 'erring' human being, we have some historical ground to believe that they might change under the pressure of changing conditions, as if in a Hegelian Dialectic, as McTaggart (Studies in Hegelian Dialectic) sees it. The difference is that it occurs in a mental-material way. The thesis, anti-thesis and the synthesis being as follows: I/we shall be the all-achieving supreme; the material pressure of overwhelmingly large population rising out of deprivation/oppression opposing it; and evolving a mid-way which to some extent serves both parties in averting the threat of extinction. And there the law of karma is supposed to get its seed to work in its natural way.

A Poet's Universe and a Philosopher[1]

ABSTRACT: Tagore's poetic vision about Man and his Universe appearing in many of his poems and other writings may be seen as reverberating the message of the Upanishads that man is One with the One Spirit and is united with the entire Universe. The sublimity of his thought in these poems and some other passages is so apparent that critics could easily see him as basically a mystic in nature delivering ideas accessible neither by reason nor by commonsense. Whether spiritualism, or for that matter, mysticism is totally averse to any kind of reason or it only transcends the latter necessitated by its own limitations, is a matter of another debate. But what prompts the following dissertation about Tagore's poetic vision is a comment of British philosopher Bertrand Russell who, once, after listening to the poet, went far ahead of others to characterize his poems as 'vague and nonsense' adding further that such things are appreciated only by Indians. It appears that while commenting so, he did not keep in mind, firstly, the history of the progress of philosophical thoughts in the world, and secondly, the fact that in Tagore's thoughts many of such philosophical thinking only naturally found their way, though in his own poetic expression. What will be more interesting to notice is that about sixty years after the date of these comments, Russell himself pleaded for some amount of 'vagueness' in a philosopher's search for the ultimate truth of the universe with the possibility of being précised later. We have not heard him change, on any later occasion, his views about Tagore with or without reference to the elaborate explanations given by the poet in his later writings to make his vision 'precise'.

[1] Previously published in The Heritage; V I, No. 2, 2015.

Introduction

A few years back, 'The Telegraph' of Calcutta in its Sunday issue of Feb 20,2011, published a feature on Nimai Chatterji, a resident of London, on his mysterious death at his residence discovered almost after four weeks by the neighbors, seated on an arm chair with hundreds of letters scattered around him. These were all written to him by the poets, authors, artists, and philosophers of his time.

Two of such letters were from the famous British philosopher Bertrand Russell with some remarks on Rabindranath Tagore. In a letter dated Feb. 16, 1963, he wrote: "I confess that his mystic air did not attract me ... He had a soft, rather elusive, manner which led me to feel that straightforward exchange or communication from which he would shy away. His intensity was impaired by his self-absorption. Naturally, his mystic views were by way of dicta and it was not possible to reason about them."

A second letter perhaps spoke more of British intolerance of that time (we shall see that it was 1912) to an Indian than of a philosopher of his stature. He wrote: "His (Tagore's) talk about the infinite is vague nonsense. The sort of language that is admired by every Indians unfortunately does not mean anything at all." (April 26, 1967).

Evidently, Russell's remarks raise a few questions. Firstly, what is a mystic vision about which no reason is possible; and secondly, whether Tagore's poetic vision was so vague as to be admired by Indians only and not by a western mind, the least by a philosopher like him. The following dissertation is an attempt to have a look into Tagore's vision of the Universe as depicted in his poems and other writings *vis-a-vis* some of the same of the western philosophers in order to ascertain how far Russell, a philosopher of outstanding reasoning, was 'reasonable' to characterize Tagore's as 'vague nonsense'.

Section I

It is almost universally believed that poets need not be philosophers in the official sense. In fact many of them are famous for their poetic vision of life and nature searching for beauty and truth in such a manner as only to create emotions to be recollected in tranquility. Those unforgettable lines of Mathew Arnold, the English poet, in the poem 'Shakespeare' go as follows: Others abide our questions, thou are free./We ask and ask – thou smilest and art still,/Out-topping knowledge.

It may appear that a poet enjoys more freedom in his effort. In the language of Tagore himself, the poet has his "... freedom from the dominance of any creed ...or in the teaching of some organized body.."[2] He has no obligation to 'justify with reason' what he says. He discovers the Truth of beauty and good, of pain and pleasure in whatever he sees by heart. One fine morning he may have a deep sense of union with the Boundless over all his limitations without any logical justification for 'what or who is the Boundless', or 'what it means to say union', etc. and sing, to quote from Tagore again from his poem 'Jivan Devata' – "..I give to thee my cup/filled with all the pain and delight/that the crushed grapes of my heart had/ surrendered,..."[3] As an explanation of this state of the mind of his, he does not give any reason. On the contrary, he writes: "You will understand from this how unconsciously I had been travelling towards the realization which I stumbled upon in an idle moment on a day in July.."[4]

And what does a philosopher do in a similar situation when he wants to know about the Universe? He takes the path of reason to understand it. He begins his search saying: "Is there any knowledge in the world which is so certain that no reasonable man could doubt it? This question, which at first sight might not seem difficult, is really

[2] Rabindranath Tagore: The Religion of Man. 2008; Rupa & Co. New Delhi, p. 78.

[3] Ibid, p. 83.

[4] Ibid, p. 84.

one of the most difficult that can be asked."[5] So, speaking generally, a philosopher's approach towards the universe fundamentally differs from that of a poet.

But there are poets who seem to pursue their life long search for a Summum Bonum which is more than mere doing poetic justice to their thoughts and feelings, a search for the inner truth of life beyond just attaining an ecstatic state of emotions fulfilled. Tagore is one of them.

If we go through the pages of his 'The Religion of Man' referred to above, where he gives elaborate interpretation of his realizations, we find that in spirit his search hardly differed from that of a philosopher.

It is true that Tagore never shied of his leanings for the mystic messages of the Upanishads. At times he supersedes worldly visions that might be read as speaking of something unreachable by reason.

In his poem 'Jivan devata' he writes- "Thou who art the innermost Spirit of my being,/art thou pleased, Lord of my Life?".[6]

Here he transcends the experience of the individual worldly self to touch the chord of the Spirit of the Upanishads as a devotee. We shall see many more occasions where Tagore is highly vocal in reverberating the messages of the Upanishads. For example, the Upanishad says:

> "He from whom proceeds all works, all desires, all odors, all tastes; who pervades all, who is beyond the senses, and in whom there is fullness of joy forever....[7] And in a poem Tagore writes: "seemaar maajhe asim tumi baajaao aapan sur, aamaar madhye tomaar prokash.....".[8] [In this poem, mention of 'asim' (the Infinite) 'tommar prakaash' (thy revelation) or later, 'kata barne

---

[5] Bertrand Russell: The Problems of Philosophy, 1959. Oxford Univ Press. London, P1.

[6] Tagore: Op. cit. p. 88.

[7] CHANDOGYA: The Upanishads 1948. New American Library, N.Y., p. 65.

[8] GEETANJALI: Poem No. 120.

kata gandhe' (in so many colors and odors) etc, only speak of the Spirit Who pervades all varieties of life]. His 'tomaar' or 'thy' is as indeterminate as 'He' of the Upanishads.

But while eulogizing the Upanishads, he also reminds us that "..our universe is the sum total of what Man feels, knows, imagines, reasons to be, and whatever is knowable to him now or in another time".[9] And also that 'Their (man's) civilization is a continual discovery of the transcendental humanity."[10] This is where Tagore takes a very different position in respect of the truth of man's universe. The phrase 'transcendental humanity' takes us, on the one hand, to the realization of the Eternal Self in every man above individual limitedness, and on the other, to the reality of mankind who progresses 'with the intimacy of a pervasive companionship'[11] with the entire Universe. That means, unlike an ordinary mystic waiting for a revelation of the otherwise unknowable, for Tagore man and his universe are the most 'living aspects' of that One Supreme Reality to reckon with.

We shall see more about it as we progress which will show that Russell's assessment about Tagore, namely, 'his mystic views were by way of dicta and it was not possible to reason about them' was inappropriate. We shall also see that western philosophers too, including Russell himself, talk of such realizations which admit that not everything is 'possible to reason about'.

Section II

As for the first question: 'What is a mystic vision that defies reason', one simple answer is this: – a person is called a mystic if he seeks to know God or some Spiritual Truth thereof through contemplation and prayer. The messages of the Upanishads are mystic in character

---

[9] Tagore. Op. Cit., p. 10.

[10] Ibid, p. 121.

[11] Ibid, p. 78.

because they say that it is not by intellect or senses but only by realizing one's own self that man reaches the highest Truth of life. When he *longs* deeply, he becomes one with the Infinite Spirit, as in prayer, uniting the entire Universe into One. This One is Brahman. The MUNDAKA says: The Self is not to be known through study of the scriptures, nor through subtlety of the intellect, nor through much learning. But by him who longs for him is he known. Verily unto him does the Self reveal his true being.

Obviously such realization falls outside normal human understanding, for, firstly, neither longing nor prayer form any part of such knowledge. And secondly, what it is that 'is not to be known' and yet 'is known'? This is sheer self-contradiction. So, unless some other justifications are given, we must bear with Hume who, from his viewing the importance of man above every passion, said that such claims "arise either from the fruitless efforts of human vanity, which would penetrate into subjects utterly inaccessible to the understanding, or from the craft of popular superstitions…".[12]

But, then, what is the real nature of man's universe? G.E. Moore in his 'Some Main Problems of Philosophy' said, a general description of the Universe must include three most important kinds of things, namely, "which we know to be in it, considering how far it is likely that there are in it important kinds of things which we do not absolutely know to be in it, and also considering the most important ways in which these various kinds of things are related to one another".[13] He proceeds with a common sense view, that is, the view of a common man, on this ground that "There are… certain views about the nature of the Universe, which are held, now-a-days, by almost everybody. They are so universally held that may, I think, fairly be called the view of Common Sense."[14] Down a few more lines he again says:

---

[12] MANDUKYA: The Upanishads. Op. cit, p. 48.

[13] D. Hume: Enquires Concerning Human Understanding, 2nd Ed. 1902, Oxford, pp. 9–11.

[14] G.E. Moore: Some Main Problems of Philosophy 1953. George Allen & Unwin. London, p. 1, 15. Ibid, p. 2.

"....The most important views of common sense: things which we all commonly assume to be true about the Universe and which we are sure that we know to be true about it."[15] ensure that things we know cannot be doubted.

But Berkeley (1685–1753) did. In fact Berkeley unseated all previous theories about the reality of man's universe, beginning with the views of Plato of 5th Century B.C. [that, only *ideas as created by God* really exist in the universe, and things of the world that we see (have *opinion* about) are their appearances][16] coming down to that of 17th century John Locke (that those things of our knowledge that come to us through *simple ideas* do really exist out there).[17]

Berkeley rejected all these and said that, things exist only as they are perceived. In his *Three Dialogues between Hylas and Philonous, in Opposition to Sceptics and Atheists,* Philonous gives to Hylas the example of two hands, hot and cold, simultaneously put in water, finding 'in reality' the same water cold and hot respectively, which is contradiction and paradoxical in term and denies existence of anything other than what mind perceives.[18]

But Moore rejects this view for the simple reason that it contradicts Common Sense. According to him, in a sensation of blue, to say that 'blue' and the 'sensation of blue' are the same is self-contradictory.[19] (Evidently the use of 'of' shows that 'sensation' and 'blue' are different)·

Berkeley's view is, however, rejected on many other grounds of which the most formidable one is that, if every body's world is as they perceive, then how does one communicate with another about

---

[15] Ibid, p. 2.

[16] B. Russell: The History of Western Philosophy, 1972. Touchstone Book, N.Y., pp. 121–22.

[17] Ibid, p. 612.

[18] George Berkeley: Three Dialogues between Hylas and Philnous, 1713; William & John Inny. London. First Dialogue.

[19] G.E. Moore: The Refutation of Idealism 1903. Mind 12.

anything, say, a table, when one in his library, reading a book on it, may see it as 'a study-room article' and another, a carpenter, who sells it, as 'a product of timber'? Moreover, when the reader uses the table in the day, leaves it in the locked library room for the night and finds the table in place the next morning, is it the same table there or they are two different tables as are perceived? The latter is ridiculous for any understanding. But if it is the same, how did it continue to exist unperceived by any one in that locked room? Berkeley had a queer answer. He said, the table exists in God's perception and that God's consciousness provides necessary communication about the table between men. Naturally he invited the next chain of insurmountable questions, namely, in whose perception did (does) God exist?, etc. We shall see, talking apparently from a similar point of view, Tagore had an answer to this problem without Berkeley's infinite regress.

Meanwhile, faced with these problems, philosophers started to talk about transcending human understanding to reach the Reality which is Thought *per excellence*, i.e. is complete in itself without being of this or that. Hegel is one of them who, being a non-Indian, tells us in a very 'Indian way(!)' that Absolute Idea or Spirit is the only reality of the universe and that things and beings we see are, as Russell presents, "our partial and erroneous ways of apprehending Reality."[20]

In fact, down the entire history of the western philosophy, this problem of mind and matter with respect to man's universe persisted until philosophers started to look at the phenomenon from an entirely different point of view. We shall come to that later (in Section III).

But before that, let us reiterate that to speak of 'Absolute Idea as wholly spiritual' is not as 'unreasonable' as Russell's earlier comments might have suggested. In fact, Russell himself commented on Hegel's believing in an 'eternal perfect unchanging spiritual unity' as "In

[20] Russell: The History etc. Op. cit., p. 734.

this conception, there is undeniably something sublime, something to which we could wish to yield assent".[21] He, however, cautioned that Hegel's arguments involve 'much confusion and many unwarrantable assumptions'. But, most significantly, this shows that the so called vague thinking of some Ultimate Truth of man's life and his universe as 'sublime spiritual' was not the monopoly of the Indians and for that matter, of Tagore. And secondly, Russell himself, sixty years after he wrote all these about Hegel and also about Tagore [the year was 1912 when in his book mentioned above he wrote about Hegel and also the year when he met Tagore[22]], started to work on his 'logical atomism' theory to show, like Wittgenstein, that the world consists not of things or objects as we know but of propositions which at their roots again have their atomic forms only. His theory of logical atomism says, those atoms are arrived at as the' last residue' in the analysis of propositions. He was, however, afraid that such 'atomic facts' might appear 'vague and ambiguous'.[23] So he wrote: "I think vagueness is very much more important in the theory of knowledge... Everything is vague to a degree you do not realize till you have tried to make it precise.."[24]

What an irony ! Russell was pleading for vagueness not to be discarded at its very sight but to wait till it was made precise. In the next section we shall see how Tagore made his vision of Unity of *Self, the selves and their Universe* '**precise**' in Russell's sense.

Section III

In this section we shall try to answer the second of our initial questions. Anyone can see that Tagore was highly inspired by the

---

[21] Russell: The Problem etc. Op. cit., p. 83.

[22] Ray Monk: Bertrand Russell – The Spirit of Solitude; 1872–1921. [Ch. 10. The Scattered Wave] 1996, Free Press. N.Y, p. 273 [Note: There is a reference of Dickinson, a Tagore admirer, who took Tagore to meet Russell in the Summer of 1912].

[23] Russell: The Philosophy of Logical Atomism, 2010. Routledge.London, pp. 3–4.

[24] Ibid, p. 4.

Upanishads in respect of Man's life and his Universe in many of his writings, particularly the poems of 'Geetaanjali', of 'Naivedya' and many others, along with an exhaustive interpretation of those visions given in his 'The Religion of Man'. But at the same time we also see that, in contrast to the spirit of the Upanishads, he had a lot of deliberations in support of his vision in the last named book.

Firstly, about the influence as told above in those poems and writings, we find that he speaks directly of the truth of some Eternal Spirit finding expression in his mind in sublimation of all kinds of reason or active apprehension. In the poem 'antara mama bikasita karo/antaratara he/........jukta karo he sabaar sange...' [25], or in this piece of writing "...on the surface of our being we have the ever-changing phases of the individual self, but in the depth there dwells the Eternal Spirit of human unity beyond our direct knowledge."[26] We can find many more of this kind of writings which show that he was by belief a mystic.

But there are many other passages in the same book and elsewhere which show that in spite of this mystic leaning for a 'Super Self' superseding 'individual' in man, he believed that ultimately all these are means to the realization of the truth of the Universe which, after all, to use Wittgenstein's phrase 'that is the case' (or the most natural truth of life). Here let us, once again, recall his words above "..our universe is the sum total of what Man feels, etc".[27] These words mean, for him, neither man nor his mental activities are surrendered for anything, be it the Indeterminate Brahman or else.

But while saying 'what Man feels etc.', did he invite again the impasse of Berkeley's 'isolation' of individual worlds? That it was far from that, becomes evident in the very next paragraph. He writes, and this is very significant, *"I do not imply that the final nature of the world depends upon the comprehension of the individual persons. Its*

---

[25] Tagore: GEETANJALI; Poem No. 5.

[26] Russell: The Problem etc. Op. Cit., p. 5.

[27] The Religion, p. 10.

reality is associated with the universal human mind which comprehends all time and all possibilities of realization. And that is why for the accurate knowledge of things we depend upon Science that represents the rational mind of the universal Man..."[28] Perhaps these lines explain more than required his unique 'vision of man's universe' eulogizing the message of the Upanishads in the light of *rationality and science.* In fact, all truths of life must appeal to this 'universal human mind' who unites in thought every individual man. But this universal Man is neither God (of Berkeley) nor the 'Indeterminate Brahman' (of the Upanishads). On the contrary, it is the ***all pervading rationality***. In fact this explains the impersonal truths of sciences which depend on ultimately appealing to humanity in the sense of organizing 'into rational concepts those facts which man can know and understand...'[29]

Thus, we may say, in all his deliberations in and through his vast world of creation he never lost sight of the fact that **Truth** shines only to a rational as well as a scientific mind, only with this rejoinder that it has to be organized by a universal mind.

Of the many stalwarts of the world who were path-breakers in the history of mankind in their respective field, Tagore had the privilege of direct interactions with Albert Einstein. Explaining the existence of the 'table' when nobody sees it, Einstein disagreed with Tagore's point that it exists for and through a universal humanity. He, on the contrary said: "...we attribute to truth a superhuman objectivity. It is indispensable for us- this reality which is independent of our existence and our experience and our mind- though we cannot say what it means."[30] He also said "...it is a belief which nobody can lack."[31] [*It would be interesting to cite a few lines from their conversation that took place between them in this respect:*

[28] Ibid, p. 11.

[29] Ibid, p. 7.

[30] Einstein and Tagore: Journal of Consciousness Studies (Controversies in Science and the Humanities), Vol. 2, 1995. Thorverton.UK.

[31] Ibid.

- **Tagore:** The world is a human world—the scientific view of it is also that of the scientific man….

  Einstein: Truth, then, or beauty, is not independent of man !

  T: No………

  E: I agree with regard to this conception of beauty, but not with regard to truth.

  T: Why not? Truth is realized through man.

  E: I cannot prove my conception is right, but that is my religion.]

We notice that, Einstein's uses of the words 'though we cannot say what it means', 'a belief which nobody can lack',' I cannot prove' etc. come very near to saying that there are some truths which are 'believed but not proved'. Moreover, to say 'nobody can lack' ultimately comes to saying 'man universally does it'.

So when Tagore said that truth absolutely unrelated to humanity is non-existent, Einstein replied: "Then I am more religious than you are."[32] That means, at times man needs a religious sort of postulations (though not religious dogma of some creed) to break some barrier.

In fact, the way Einstein was explaining his ground for the belief in the truth of an independent world outside man's domain going ahead of logic and scientific reasoning compares very closely to Tagore's vision of it in the sense, there is always the scope for a creative imagination to overtake mechanical reasoning. With reference to the creative spirit of man, Tagore writes: "It is the consciousness in Man of his own creative personality which has ushered in this new regime in Life's kingdom".[33]

So, whether a poet or a philosopher or in this particular sense a scientist, all are in search of the ultimate truth of the Universe as it is. We do not know as yet if the last word is said in this respect. But Tagore seems to have kept himself alive to it all along even when some philosophers started to say that the traditional approach

---

[32] Ibid.

[33] Tagore: The Religion etc. Op. Cit., p. 29.

to this problem is inadequate. They came up with completely a new version of the world which, according to them, would provide the required passage from the knower to the world there. So when Tagore's Hibbert Lectures of 1930 was published as 'The Religion of Man', L. Wittgenstein, a stalwart of Vienna Circle, was already at the centre stage of the new movement with his Tractatus Logico-philosophicus (1920). And it is most unlikely that Tagore had no idea of it. So it attracts our question if his vision had anything in common with the new movement too.

Leaving the question of independent objects of the world behind, Wittgenstein voiced his new thoughts from the very first assertion in the Tractatus, the long introduction of which was written by his teacher and friend Russell himself. Some of them could be restated here to see if any of them could be interesting from Tagore's point of view.

The first assertion is: "The World is that is the case." (T.1). This is followed by "The world is the totality of facts, not of things". (T 1.1), and then, a few assertions later: "The facts in logical space are the world". (T 1.13).[Let us note that all his assertions are within a frame of inclusive number series, indicating that the truth of each lies in some relation to the totality structure of it, which we shall see was purposefully done to show the truth of his view that the world can be stated only in a framework of propositions.]

As we proceed, we know what the phrase 'that is the case' means. He says: "What is the case - fact- is the existence of states of affairs" (T 2). That means, 'facts' are not 'things' (like tables, brown, books, etc, of the world as they are), but the 'states of affairs', which are of the simplest relational form of propositions, such as, 'table-colored-brown' 'books-on the-table' and so on. (*Note:* 'colored' or 'on the' stand for a 'relations' making table, brown, and book the 'states of affairs'). And there are no table or brown or book as such. They exist only so far they are part of a state of affairs.

But what asserts the existence of the states of affairs? He says: (T 4.21) - "The simplest kind of proposition, an elementary proposition, asserts the existence of a state of affairs".

Now, as to the most relevant question, what from out side the proposition makes it true, Wittgenstein says: "A proposition is a truth-function of elementary propositions. (An elementary proposition is a truth-function of itself)" [T 5]. That means, a proposition (i.e. man's sole means of knowledge) is true if its constituent elementary propositions are true, whereas truth of an elementary proposition depends on itself only, not anything outside it. There is thus no question of infinite regress. According to Wittgenstein, the world is not materially produced by things or objects as they are, but is constructed by propositions "with the help of a logical scaffolding..." (T 4.023).

Now, what we find in Tagore's vision of the Universe is not very different from this contention that so called *reality* is nothing but some universally accepted (like, 'that is the case') form of consciousness. We come across a striking similarity of this in these words of Tagore: "...reality is not based in the substance of things but in the principle of relationship. ...Reality is human; it is what we are conscious of, by which we are affected, that which we express".[34] For the poet, the world is the totality of these 'relationships occurring in consciousness' (a proposition for Wittgenstein?) of the universal man.

Incidentally Wittgenstein realized that these hundreds of assertions did not take him to where he wanted to reach and confessed in the last two of them that—"He (his follower) must transcend these propositions, and then he will see the world aright" (T 6.54) and "What we cannot speak about we must pass over in silence" (T 7). Does Tagore face a similar problem? Perhaps not, for, the poet in him can easily say "...reality is the definition of the infinite which relates truth to the person."[35] The question of transcendence comes when we think of knowing efforts of finite individuals. On the other hand, Man who represents the universal man, lives with the Universe without effort. [viswa saathe joge jethaye vihaara/sei khane jog tomaar saathe aamaro....";[36] which says, the universe

[34] Ibid, p. 120.

[35] Ibid, p. 120.

[36] Tagore: GEETANJALI; Poem No. 94.

where the Universal Man treads is where the person of the poet too steps with].

Concluding Remarks

In course of our deliberation above, we have tried to drive at a few points. Firstly, whatever does not fit into the frame of formal logic and reason, may not be discarded as vague and nonsense for such hasty effort falls short of exhausting all possible means of knowledge. Secondly, in spite of his strong bond with the mysticism of the Upanishads highlighting the abode of a Supreme Spirit in Man, Tagore had his own vision sufficiently distanced from the former's indeterminate character through reason and extremely comprehensive poetic vision.

Thirdly, as for our knowledge about the Universe, scientific as well as philosophical enquiry take us a long way, but not to such length as to provide a full proof answer for all related questions. We have seen Einstein's view too. And also of Wittgenstein. In the Tractatus, the most important event of 20th century (as termed by Russell in his introduction), he had to accede a possible transcendence in man's knowing effort in this respect. In fact, Russell himself expressed realizations about the limits of philosophical knowledge (Ch. 14 of The Problems…) at the same time when he expressed a different opinion about Tagore.

And, fourthly, attempts to reach the truth of man and his universe *beyond* the laid-down paths of knowledge has always been with the philosophers through ages. So, if Tagore spoke about one of such means, he cannot be blamed by anyone, and the least by a philosopher.

But all said, he was above all a poet, and his vision poetic. His Universe is so comprehensive in nature that his thoughts have something for all, including philosophers. Only an adequate preparedness is required to appreciate it.

Motivation and the State of Liberation[1]

I

In Indian scriptures, as also in its different philosophical systems, there is mention of an important state of the life of a man, the ultimate one that man can aspire to achieve, called Moksa. It is the state where man is 'liberated', meaning, where he is free from all 'attachments towards something one desires to happen to him in his worldly life'. On the other hand, the science of mind and body says, man's action towards achieving something is possible only when he is so motivated by the thought that he desires (or is interested) to see it happen to him.

Again, the Gita says, man must always be motivated to do some work to achieve his continuity (i.e. survival), for, otherwise his biological existence will be at stake. ["niyatam kuru karma tvam… sharirayaatraapi ca … etc. Sec.III. 8]. It also says, the pure soul is he who works without any motive, i.e. for whom achieving and non-achieving do not bear any difference. ["…. Siddhi asiddhyoh nirvikaarah kartaa…" Sec. XVIII, 26].

The question that becomes imminent from the above is: how the two phenomena described in the two preceding paragraphs respectively, namely, those about moksa and motivation in the former, and the two messages of the Gita in the latter, go together? This in fact makes the principal ground for the materialists to question the concept of moksa advocated by Indian Scriptures and philosophical systems following them.

---

[1]Previously published in Maha Milan: V. 26, No. 8, 2018.

Mokṣa or liberation is said to be a state of dissociation of the *soul* from the body of worldly affairs. But what is this *soul* over and above the mind-body a person perceives of himself in his day to day life? Almost all the systems of Indian Philosophy, except the Materialist system of Cārvāka, believe that it is the highest state of human life. Even the Buddhists who uphold the doctrine of 'No Soul' i.e. no spiritual self beyond human life, do admit liberation or nirvāṇa or state of overcoming the bondage of life as the supreme end of human life. In fact, the Hindu Ethics, as envisaged by the Vedas and Manusmrti, underline Four Purusharthas as the goal of human life, namely, Dharma, Artha, Kaama and Moksa.

The present treatise is concerned mainly with the concept of Moksa or liberation, the fourth of the Purusharthas, to see, on the one hand, whether it is consistent to say that the same man who pursues the first three as his worldly goals also pursues the fourth that takes him away from his worldly aspirations; and on the other, whether the materialists are right to think that the concept of man's liberation or moksa (in their words, a man achieving the so-called state of 'no perceivable state of man' i.e. 'No-Man') directly contradicts the principle of motivation in which man works to achieve only such 'goal' that is perceivably desired to happen to him.

II

By the word 'man', I mean the 'man as we commonly come across' in our day-to-day life who eats, drinks, makes merry, also longs for more. In this sense, my concept of man as the 'common man' is not just a helpless onlooker in the midst of endless events of the world occurring around him as was portrayed by the legendary Indian cartoonist Laxman, but is one who also strives to achieve something to make his life better and better. In fact, it is this thought of betterment working as the driving force, i.e. this 'motivation' that separates him from other creatures.

Going by the messages of the Indian Philosophical thinkers, we learn that, Indian wisdom through ages never contented with 'knowledge of the right work for betterment' only, but tried to seek through it the highest form of this betterment of man's life in this world itself. The Vedic concept of 'Purushaartha' or man's 'journey' as the achiever of his goals in life [prescribed in the Ethics of Hinduism and in the messages of Manusmrti (2nd Century BCE)] speaks of a living that passes through four stages, namely, *dharma, artha, kaama* and *moksa*. The Dharma way of life means 'righteousness or pursuing moral values in life'. That of Artha means 'prosperity or attaining economic values of the deeds one performs'. And that of Kaama on the other hand is to attach equal value to what one needs for his biological living, namely, 'pleasure, love, procreation, etc that add to one's psychological satisfactions too'. In another sense, this also means the fulfillment of man's worldly existence.

But the fourth of the Purushaarthas, namely *Mokṣa* or liberation, has been considered as the state of the highest good or *summumbonum* of life in contrast to the other three. It is a state of spiritual excellence or the true self whereas the other three Purushaarthas appear to be 'māyā' or perceivably satisfying 'lower order' goal of life'. They are said to have no independent value, nor they are of permanent nature, for, each is oriented as the way of life demands them, depending on the constantly changing worldly situations. Only 'Moksa' is a state of achievement where all seeking of man's common living are drowned into 'fruitlessness' and the limited achievements thereby are surrendered for the permanent state of eternal bliss. It is the state where only the 'pure and unattached soul' prevails leaving behind all other material seeking of life, including pleasure pain, the act of judging good or bad of an action, and the like. Thus, while all other states concern the mortal self, the state of Moksa is 'immortality achieved'. There is no 'I know this', 'I know that'; nor 'I have this', 'I want that .... 'and the like, for, there is no separate 'I', but the 'self which is Pure consciousness without any differentiation with what is achieved'.

A great disciple of the Upanishads, one of the treasure of Indian philosophical thoughts, pointed at the inexplicable nature of the latter (namely, Self) asking her teacher husband: "Where there is only consciousness of the Self and individuality is no more, this that you say my lord, confuses me". [Maitreyi Yaanabalka in Brihadaaranyaka Upanishad, The Upanishads, New American Library. 1957]. This is the question that every common man shall ask pointing to more than one doubts. Firstly, if all the aforesaid Purushaarthas are the four goals of human life, than how the fourth one shall mean the negation of the first three concerning the same worldly man's living? Secondly, a man may live a good moral life, can accumulate wealth in a rightful way (that is, without stealing, without depriving anybody, and so on), can satisfy lust within the limits of social sanctions. In every case, it is an 'I' or an individual 'X' who achieves the goal. The identity of the individual is retained in each case. Had there been no body or no 'I-feeling', then such 'achievements' would cease to have any meaning for him. And, if the fourth Purushaartha is a goal to be pursued by the same man, then how it is possible that he would be interested to achieve something where he *himself* will not be there? Again, thirdly, if 'purusha' means 'man', and 'artha' means 'the goal', then, however higher the state of 'moksa' may be, the role of the purusha who has to 'see' (perceive) that it all really happens to him cannot be abandoned even at that state without contradiction.

If, however, it is claimed that, 'purusha' in reality means the 'self' which in essence is detached from all worldly parameters, then the other three purusharthas become self-defeating. A detached self cannot be an aspiring purusha for objects of attachment like pleasure etc. Moreover, why 'he', the man so much working for the goal, should be dropped in that state while he can happily live with it in the other three?

It is said, the other three purushaarthas are limited in nature and are not permanent, for, they are aimed at such goals that the mind-body form of the 'self' can perceive as really achievable in his worldly life, while the fourth is a permanent state of 'unlimited nature'. In that state remains no limited individual as 'I' or 'Me' to gain or lose anything that matters for his worldly life; no 'I' to take pleasure or pain at anything. In a state of moksa or liberation, there is only pure unattached consciousness.

But, we shall see that Indian wisdom, the Gita in particular, does not take 'liberation' as a state of abandoning all that matters for day to day leaving of a common man. On the contrary, the message of 'Purushaartha' itself says that it is like the other three goals that only man of this world can aspire to achieve. We shall also see that pursuing a 'liberated life 'is not sundered from all kinds of activities (i.e. all kinds of motivations), though, however, like the other three purushaarthas there are no emotions like that of happiness or remorse on corresponding success and failure, on doing good or bad, on gain or loss, on being loved or hated etc.

But before that let us see why the view of the materialists rejecting the very concept of moksa is not tenable.

III

The Cārvākas, the materialist school of Indian Philosophy, which apparently may be taken as the common man's view, oppose the concept of liberation on the ground that such a 'state of existence of man is a myth' because in practical life man never perceives a substance other than this mind-body reality, neither of him nor of any other man. Their argument against such concept may be simple. Those who believe in the possibility of such a state of life in which the person in such state is not what we ordinarily perceive of a worldly man, may do so on two grounds, both of which are untenable. Let us see what such grounds can be and how they may be refuted by the materialists.

One of the grounds for believing in the state of moksa may be as follows: The process of improvement of the life of a man occupying this perceivable world is an endless one. From birth to death it is only progresses towards a better and still better a life that sustains it. It, therefore, cannot stop at some point to say, without contradiction, 'no better state'. That means, they would argue, if we believe in man's continued growth-process, which is a reality for his survival as a natural species, it logically supersedes the limits of whether or not a state so realized by a person is perceived or perceivable as a state of this world. The liberated 'soul' can be 'reality' by its own truth even if it is not perceived to fit this world pattern of man.

The second argument: Moksa is a state where the individual self is at the highest label and is transformed into pure consciousness. At this state, the 'I of worldly existence' is freed from all worldly predications, i.e. not known through any study....nor through learning of any kind. It is known only by him who longs for him. Verily unto him does the Self *reveal* his true being. [*Mandukya Upanishad.* The Upanishads. New American Library]. In other words, the truth of a liberated soul can only be 'revealed' to the liberated one without being in the form of knowing a proposition to be true [as in 'I know that..etc'] and therefore cannot be known by any usual means of knowledge, the least by perception.

The Carvaka refutes both the arguments on the ground that the possibility of knowledge 'without being perceptual' is a myth. No true statements about something can be made if it is not based on perception.

Their principal argument for refutation of non-perceptual means of knowledge may be stated as follows: when, for example, we arrive at some knowledge of the form 'S is P' [such as 'It is raining' about a particular state of the nature], in one occasion by perception and in another by inference, the latter can always be doubted, whereas there is no scope of doubt in the former. Who can doubt the experience of his he faces in rains while walking in it with or without his umbrella open? But for one who utters the same statement sitting in a room and not in a position to look outside, inferring the same from the sound he hears of the drops of water, the truth of his statement can very well be doubted. For example, the basis of his inference that 'All cases of falling sound of water drops are cases of rain' can be questioned because, in this case, such sounds might have been artificially produced the fire fighters, opening their hose to facilitate a film shooting of a rainy scene, etc.

Now, if so doubted, the inference 'S is P' as a piece of valid knowledge can be accepted only after its truth is verified. But the question that arises, can we verify it by a non-perceptual knowledge, say, another inference without begging the question?

Let us see how it happens. The verification process may be formulated as follows:

1. One person A says, (a) '*there is q (it is raining), because there is p (sound of rain drops heard), and p always entails q.*' ['There is q' is an inferential knowledge]
2. Another person B asks, how do you know that *p* always entails *q*?
3. A replies: Because *(b) 'p is always caused by q. And since there is p, its cause q must have been there'.*
4. Again B asks, how do you know that *p is always caused by q?*
5. A replies: Because (*c*) '*p* and *q* are causally related and, as a law, *p cannot be caused without q'.*

This being circularity of argument and, therefore, inconclusive, we can refer to another supporting law. But that will again be inconclusive for the truth of (c) for the same reason of circularity, such as (d) '*no effects can take place without being preceded by its cause'.* This is how we are dragged to begging the question because the truth of this law too is what we have already doubted. This can be avoided only if any of the laws is shown true without doubt, and what can remove doubt about the truth of a statement other than actual instances supporting it? And only perceptual knowledge can do that.

In fact, this is the actual procedure that is followed in *anumana* or inferential knowledge adopted by the Nyaya system of Indian philosophy substantiating a *vyāpti* or the truth of the general premise (the law) by reference to actual cases so perceived. On the basis of perceptual support '*p,* therefore *q*' is deduced. [The steps are termed as *udaaharana and nigamana]*. But since all cases of past present and future referred by the general premise or law cannot be perceptually verified, hence the validity of inferential knowledge remains always doubtful.

So, the materialists argue, no heaven or hell beyond this life. Such things can only be matter of imagination or of some other form of non-perceptual knowledge, not substantiated by perception. The 'Self' beyond the worldly mind-body or the one in the so-called state of moksa are all baseless imaginations and to be abandoned for good. Man's only motto should be to fulfill all his desires of worldly life for that is only what one can 'know' as true.

Secondly, who can be motivated to aspire for such a thing as 'liberation' which does not bear any fruits for his life that practically matters for him? After all, one can be motivated to achieve only such things what he can 'see' as actually happening to his liking.

And thirdly, if liberation means absolute freedom from pain, meaning thereby, there shall be no miseries at all, then it would be an absurd thinking having no real existence. Human life is a bundle of mixed perceptions having both pain and pleasure, because all states of pleasure are built upon some worldly conditions conducive to it at that moment, and so is always overcast by the fear of change in that condition. To attain a state where there is only 'unbound pleasure' and no 'fear' i.e. no pain, is an impossible state of 'un-conditionality' falling outside the scope of perceptual truth. In fact, human beings can only aspire to have minimum pain and to enjoy maximum pleasure under one particular condition. A good life is a life of maximum enjoyment in this life itself because only that much he can see to truly happen to him.

The Chārvakas are the hedonists of Indian Philosophy according to whom the view regarding 'soul' or 'Spiritual Self' of the Vedas and the Upanishads is nothing but denying the 'body' that is the only thing perceived. It is this body which works with conscious behavior – '*Caitanyaviśiṣtadeha*'. If this body is sundered from its experiences, it ceases to exist. Hence, if Liberation means complete cessation of all human experiences pertaining to emotions of pain, pleasure, sufferings, joy, etc, which are inseparable from his bodily existence, then it can only mean death where 'he' is '*no-body*'. And nobody can be motivated to achieve something which '*he (that is, his bodily existence) does not remain to see*'.

Now, the materialism of the carvaka has been rejected on many grounds. The chief of it is aimed at their main argument that perception is the only valid source of knowledge, and that since we perceive nothing beyond this worldly 'bodied existence' as mentioned above, there can be no such state of this body where it is 'no-body'.

Here we shall mention one ground which will show that their claim of 'only perception' is untenable. In fact, perception itself involves 'unperceived elements', better known as *inferential elements*, to complete its function as a means of knowledge. I have made use of this argument of 'inferential element' as a theory of 'construction in perception' in the chapter entitled "Argument for A Higher Life of The Common Man", in the present collection. Here Let us examine an example where 'seeing' may be seen implicitly performing the act of ***'using a vyāpti or general premise'***, like an inferential knowledge, ***as the basis of*** what is perceived.

Supposing a person, who believes that perception is the only source of valid knowledge, is walking for a long time in a jungle through trees, mounds of termites etc. He eventually becomes thirsty but bears with his thirst instead of rushing to the trees or the mounds, he sees, to quench it. Why?

Because he sees these objects as 'trees and mounds that do not quench thirst'.

Suddenly he comes across a pot of water. This time he rushes to that. Why?

Because he sees that object as 'water which is a quencher of thirst'.

It can be seen that, in both cases, namely 'seeing trees and mounds as not to quench his thirst', and 'seeing water as the quencher of thirst', he relies on some truth which involves 'un-perceived' elements, namely, the 'inferential elements', such as the knowledge of general laws. In the first instance, it is the truth of a 'generalized premise' (obviously falling outside the field of perception of particulars) that "No cases of trees or mounds are conducive to quenching of thirst"; and in the second, "All cases of water in a pot (eligible for drinking of course) are cases of quenching of thirst by drinking". And such generalized laws are the ones that are used as the basis of inference, for example, in the case of knowing fire perceiving an instance of smoke ["All cases of smoke are cases of fire", etc.].

Thus we may say, perception cannot independently be a source of valid knowledge; it must give way to other indirect forms of knowledge to facilitate it. And thus said, 'the state of the soul as liberated' cannot be rejected on the ground that such a state is not perceived.

And about their argument that human motivation is always driven by the thought of achieving this or that goal of this world only and therefore cannot go side by side with his striving for 'something' that achieves nothing of this world, it may be said that, the advocates of the state of moksa do not say that attaining liberation means cessation of everything of this life. A liberated soul still continues to see the truths of life and his role in it though only in a different way. We can refer to the messages of the Gita in this respect and see how this practically happens in the case of the ascetics or the Sanyasins who are believed to have a detached life and are seen to rush to serve men of the society in distress. Their 'motivation to relieve people from sufferings' and 'a state of total detachment from worldly motivations' can co-exist without contradiction.

IV

The Bhagavad Gita says, in a state of liberation man continues to work for the maintenance of mankind without being emotionally involved in it. In his English rendering of The Bhagavad Gita, Dr. S. Radhakrishnan interprets this as follows: "Liberation is not the isolation of the immortal spirit from the mortal human being (*our 'common man'*), but is the transfiguration of the whole man. ... His whole nature is subdued to the universal vision.." He refers to the 25th verse of Section III of the Gita which says "... vidvān tathā asaktah cikirsuh lokasmgraham", meaning, at the liberated state, there still are the activities of the pure and unburdened personality (*asaktah*) of the achiever, though not for 'him' in isolation but, for the 'holding together of the world'. Here 'lokasamgarha' means 'preserving the mankind'. Here we shall refer to the activities or service to the suffering humanity rendered by the Sanyāsins or the ascetics, particularly of India. They are believed to have achieved the highest goal, that is, the state of 'pure and free, buoyant and unburdened state of human life', and yet are driven to activities for the relief of the suffering mankind whenever such need arises.

Now regarding the role of motivation in human actions, it may be said, no conscious act (which, incidentally, is exclusive to human beings) can take place without a motive behind. That means, no one can go ahead with a particular work without fixing a specific goal to achieve by it. And working with a view to achieve something is what we call 'attachment'. Now, serving the suffering mankind when it is in distress is also a particular goal whoever aims at it, be a common man or a *sanyāsi.* So, are the liberated souls that the *sanyāsins* are believed to be, *motivated* by the thought of 'freeing one from any kind of suffering' in its usual sense? If yes, then what we see in such relief operations undertaken by the *sanyasins'* (for example, during calamities or such other necessities that may arise in the society around him) is either that the man in a liberated state is motivated like any other common man having attachment towards the goal, or activities can take place 'without motivation'. The first possibility contradicts the concept of *moksa,* and the second leads to a categorical impossibility. [Action, which needs 'motivation', is an action 'without motivation']. Let us, then, see if there is any contradiction or category mistake in thinking of man as 'being active' and 'being in a state of moksa' at the same time.

Firstly, there is no contradiction between the two, for, giving up all desires for fruits of action, as envisaged by the concept of *moksa,* does not entail giving up all actions. In fact, Gita in its Section III, Verse 4, says "*na karmanah anārambhaat ...na ca sannāsanāt eba siddhim...*", which means, 'not by abstention from work does a man attain freedom from action; nor by mere renunciation does he attain his perfection' [Tr. Radhakrishnan], because, it goes on to say, "*na hi kashcit ksanamapi jātu tisthati akarmakrit...*", meaning, no one can remain without work even for a moment, for, that is what nature demands of him. Indeed according to the Gita, only work with worldly desires are discarded, not actions that are performed where man's senses are under complete control of (pure) mind and he is free from all (worldly) attachments. In other words, one who is liberated does take to action 'with definite purpose' but only with *his pure mind keeping him free from serving his personal worldly interests.*

It may be asked, can there be a 'definite purpose' of action in this world without worldly motivation? To this we find an answer in the Gita itself. In the aforesaid section, verses 19, it introduces the phrase 'asaktah satatam kāryam karma samācara', which may be translated as 'doing what is *to be done*'. And this 'to be done' initiative of the pure mind is a kind of motivation where there is a goal but no personal drive of any of dharma artha and kama.

As to what can this goal be where there is motivation but no personal motivation, the Gita says, undertaking some action with a view to sustaining humanity is not only consistent with but mandatory (*'kartum arhasi', meaning 'bounden duty')* for one who is liberated. [*'lokasamgaham eva api sampasyan kartum arhasi* '; Ibid, Sect 20]. The phrase 'lokasamgraha' may be translated as 'working for the wellbeing of mankind so as to sustain it'; and perhaps no work can be more ensuring the wellbeing of mankind than undertaking relief work for men in distress of any kind. To help people out from the calamities of flood or drought or, say, from the pains fighting diseases like cancer is no mean a work to maintain the society, that is, 'loka'. The verse refers to Janaka, the king, who attained the state of the liberated soul by way of this kind of activities only. And king Janaka is none other than a person having features of a worldly man, i.e. a common man.

So we can say, on the one hand, that achieving a state where there remains no worldly desires and motives does not mean absolute giving up of all kinds of action or *karma*. And since action cannot be undertaken by one without motivation, hence there is no water-tight exclusivity between 'attaining the state of moksa' and 'working with a motive'. In this connection, we may refer to the 26th verse of Sect 18 of the Gita which, speaking on moksa says: *muktasangah anahambādi dhrti-utsāhasamanbitah siddhi-asiddhyoh nirvikarah karta sattbikah ucyate* (It may be translated as: whose actions are free from desire, not prompted by egoistic thoughts, where zeal and patience are in perfect synthesis, and who remains unmoved by the success or failure of the work is one who is said to have attained a pure soul of the liberated). Here the so-called 'motive for action' follows the dictates of karaniya or 'to be done' as demanded by a situation and not his 'personal motive'.

Thus, it is equally possible that by taking to worldly actions too (though of specific nature like sustaining human race, etc) one can attain *siddhi* or liberation. Rather we may say, if human race is not liberated from the limitations of the world causing pains and miseries, no one is 'individually liberated' in the real sense, for, he is a part of this human race. About this truth of 'the path of liberation', Swami Vivekananda says "During my Sadhana period ... what strenuous efforts had I made for my spiritual practices ! But now I have not that thirst for liberation. My present mood is that so long as one individual lives in this world without gaining liberation, I do not want my own liberation. (Reminiscences of Swami Vivekananda: Kolkata, Advaita Ashrama.2004. pp. 325-26).

Now, regarding our question as to how do the sanyāsins who are supposed to have attained liberation 'work' like any other motivated work of ordinary man to organize a relief work for man in distress, the Gita in its Sec V entitled 'sanyāsayoga' or the path of being liberated, verse 11, says that, even when one is liberated, he does not cease to work in the worldly sense, for his sense organs and motor organs still remain active in him. Its difference with an ordinary activity out of worldly motivation is that, here the activities take place in their natural course by the senses without involving any motivation of the soul in order attain some state (be it 'the state of liberation'). [*kevaloih indriyoih api yoginah karma kurbanti sangamtyaktbātma shuddhaye].*

Thus, coming to the question of co-existence of the concept of liberation on the one hand and 'man's engaging himself to fulfill some goal' [or more specifically, Vivekananda's following the path to liberation while vowing to work for the liberation of each and every man of the world before his own] we may refer to Radhakrishnan's interpretation of the phrase 'cikirsuh lokasamgraham' of the Gita: "Liberation is not the isolation of the immortal spirit from the mortal human life but is transfiguration of the whole man. ….His whole nature is subdued to the universal vision". In other words, man has a two-program path towards liberation: obtaining complete release from attachments and personal tensions, and doing work for the betterment of man (including total freedom from worldly adversities) in the world around at the same time. In fact, a liberated soul cannot be in the abode of his attainment when a retched fellow member the society is dying at his doorsteps in utter distress. Realizing the state of Moksa can wait, but not helping out the man in danger of extinction from life. Going forward to serve him is also part of his following the spiritual route to salvation.

In our day to day life, we see many people doing good work for other men and women or even for animals needing help. The question is, are such works conducive to taking one to the path of liberation? If such work is done for some return in future like something materially good to happen in this life or even in the life hereafter (if, however, there is any), or, may be it is not done for any material gain, but is done for some kind of fame giving emotional satisfaction in the act, or as just an act gratifying in its own, the answer is 'No'. But if it is done as a 'karaniya' or 'to be done by itself' without reference to anything 'personal', then the answer is 'YES'. The Gita says: anistam istam misranca … bhabati atyāginām pretya na tu sanyāsinām kkacit. (Sect XVIII, V 12). It means, good, bad or a mix of both are things that happen only to the former class of people, mentioned above, who are attached (to a desirable status of their life in future, may be beyond life hereafter). But to the latter, no such things happen, because, he (to whose class belong the aforesaid sanyāsins) does not work for any so-called 'future' of him.

V

So, the concept of moksa or liberation as a reality as the highest state of life cannot be ruled out as void as the materialists would claim to, and a path to it may be ensuring wellbeing of mankind. And if the latter is true, then an ascetic having attained the state of moksa can very well be motivated to ensuring it helping suffering mankind come out of distress of any kind including the one caused by natural calamity. Similarly, a common man, with all his sense-driven emotions and worldly aspirations pursuing the *purushārthas* of *kāma* and *artha* may very well be on the path to morality or *dharma* maintaining worldly observance of righteousness (of non-stealing, non-lying, non-violence, etc) and go beyond that to attain the high state of moksa if he works to help human race to survive as he himself wishes to. The last may sound unrealistic for an ordinary man, for, he is not ordinarily accustomed to thinking of mankind beyond him, more unlikely that he thinks about the maintenance of it. But that does not mean that he is unable to think about men around him. In course of interaction with them to secure his good, once he feels that 'he occupies only a small place among innumerable men and women around him ', his activities are on the path to a kind of motivation which increasingly finds itself unattached to things in isolation, i.e. to things once he thought to exclusively happen to him. We may say, there is a transition, however rudimentary, from 'only to me' to 'to me along with others' to 'to others'.

A good example of such a 'non-I' transition of 'I-only' may be observed in a man who finds him marooned by floods along with many others, waiting to be rescued. However self-seeking the man in his daily life may be, this time he cannot be rationally motivated to try for a rescue operation 'for him only', for, that is an unrealistic thinking in that particular situation. What instead he is motivated to is to seek 'rescue operation for everyone' which only shall rescue also him.

Therefore, firstly, that man cannot by nature strive for the good of others leaving aside what is usually his prime thought, namely, only his good, is not true. On the contrary, sometimes he may be motivated to perform the act of 'renunciation' as the right action to ensure his own. And, secondly, this entails that, necessity so arising, he shall also, as Swami Vivekananda said, look for others' good instead of (that is, before) his own. This marks the all-important step towards 'unattached motivation' (here the path being that of *cikirsuh lokasamgraham* sense).

Thus, we may say that, there is no contradiction between 'to be unattached' and 'to be motivated'. And, more importantly, so far the common man of the world is concerned, there is no contradiction between 'to be a common man with his worldly purusharthas of artha and kāma (and also of dharma which, however, adheres only to worldly value judgments)' and 'to pursue the path of superseding them'. The only differentiating character of such motivation in a common man is that, unlike those who solely devote themselves to attaining that state of 'freedom' (or 'being unattached'), he might have to wait for the right moment for it to come to him in some form or other.